The Enneagram Made Simple

THE ENNEAGRAM

MADE SIMPLE

A No-Nonsense Guide to Using
the Enneagram for Growth and Awareness

ASHTON WHITMOYER-OBER, MA

ROCKRIDGE
PRESS

For general information on our other products and services or to obtain technical support, please contact our Customer Care Department within the United States at (866) 744-2665, or outside the United States at (510) 253-0500.

Rockridge Press publishes its books in a variety of electronic and print formats. Some content that appears in print may not be available in electronic books, and vice versa.

Interior and Cover Designer: Elizabeth Zuhl
Art Producer: Samantha Ulban
Editor: Eun H. Jeong
Production Editor: Ellina Litmanovich
Production Manager: Eric Pier-Hocking

Author Photo Courtesy of Aubree Shannon Photography

Paperback ISBN: 978-1-63807-299-7 | eBook ISBN: 978-1-63807-691-9
R0

To Preston. May you always seek to
understand yourself and those around you.
My life began the day you were born.

CONTENTS

INTRODUCTION

I think it's a natural human instinct to want to know more about ourselves. We want to understand who we are, why we are like this, how we got here, and how we can move forward. We strive to know ourselves a little bit more today than we did yesterday. Enter the Enneagram.

The Enneagram is a personality typing system that consists of nine different "types." It differs from other personality typing systems in that it doesn't describe our behaviors. There are stereotypical behaviors that align with each of the nine types, but the Enneagram is about our motivations: the why and how behind what we do. We all may exhibit the same behaviors, but the motivations behind those behaviors are often very different. Those motivations are what delineate the nine different types.

I have always been extremely interested in personality tests. Growing up in my family, we went to our local bookstore every Thursday night. (We would only get to go to the bookstore if my sister and I got along that week, though.) The bookstore was such a treat, and probably why I'm still mesmerized by bookstores today. As soon as we arrived, I would race to the back of the store, straight to the psychology and personality section. Even at a young age, I was trying to figure out who I was. I took all kinds of personality tests, from trying to figure out my Myers-Briggs type to discovering which Disney princess I was. (Cinderella, in case you're wondering.)

Fast-forward to college, when I decided to venture into the psychology world for my higher education. There I kept learning about different personality typing systems, but it was always the same story. These personality tests explained *who* you were, but then you were just left with that information, with no real useful guidance for how to move forward. While pursuing my master's degree in psychology, I discovered the Enneagram. *This* was the answer to all my prior questions about other personality tests. It told me what kind of person I was, but more importantly, it told me *why* and then guided me on how I can change my behavior and engage with the world in a better way. I became enamored with the Enneagram and knew that I wanted to share this information with others.

Today I am a community psychologist, certified Enneagram coach, and author on the subject, among other things. It may sound dramatic, but the Enneagram has changed my life. Now that I know why I do things (and why others behave in a certain way), I'm able to understand more about myself and others. I'm able to adjust some of those behaviors that I don't love and use this information to grow deeper into who I really am. I became certified in the Enneagram so I could share this knowledge with others who want to learn more. I hope this book and the information in it changes your life as much as it did mine.

HOW TO USE
THIS BOOK

Through this book, you will learn the basics of the Enneagram, discovering the nine "types" of people and how they engage with the world. I provide exercises for each type to help you nurture your growth or change some of the behaviors you might not like. You will begin with a self-assessment that will help you discover what type you are and start you on your own Enneagram journey to becoming your best self. You may also want to take an Enneagram test that is available on the Internet. You can find such tests at The Enneagram Institute and Truity. However, it's important not to rely solely on these tests to determine your type. Here's why.

Tests are sometimes great at getting to some of those stereotypical behaviors associated with each type, but not necessarily what is motivating you to behave that way. In addition, if we're truly honest with ourselves, sometimes we answer questions in ways that we want other people to perceive us. We're human. It's okay, but that's why the Enneagram can be a journey. We love quick fixes and for someone to tell us who we are, but in order for the Enneagram to be beneficial, you need to first sit with each of the types and see what resonates. Look at the core fears and desires of all nine types and truly be honest with yourself about why you do the things you do. From there, you can do the work to see real change occur in your growth.

Because the Enneagram is about motivations, not behaviors, this means that once we know what motivates us to act the way that we do, we can step into that realization and either embrace those behaviors or change them. Think of it as nine different ways of viewing the world. Based on our Enneagram type, we view situations through a specific lens. It's like each type is wearing a different colored lens to view the world. For example, let's pretend that all Enneagram Ones are wearing blue-colored glasses, whereas all Enneagram Threes are wearing green-colored glasses. Ones and Threes could be looking at the same situation, but Ones will see it with a blue tint and Threes will see it with a green tint. Becoming aware of the different types helps us become more aware about ourselves and come to understand the different relationships in our lives.

I encourage you to go into this book with an open mind, ready to take in the information. Don't assume that you are a specific type; instead, confirm it while reading this book. This book is a starting point, and your journey is just beginning.

PART I

ABCs of the Enneagram

In this part of the book, we'll dive into what the Enneagram is and what the word means. We're going to discuss the history of the Enneagram, all the terminology you'll need to know, and how to discover your own Enneagram type without the use of a traditional test. We're also going to talk about the symbol itself, what all the lines mean, and how we're all connected to more than one Enneagram type.

CHAPTER 1

Explaining the Enneagram

CONCEPTION

The Enneagram has been around for a long time, making it difficult to pinpoint exactly where and how it began. Most theories contend that the Enneagram was created to enhance spirituality. This doesn't necessarily mean Christianity, although some Christian organizations and individuals have used the Enneagram in their teachings. A common misconception is that the Enneagram is only for those who identify with the Christian faith, and that just isn't the case. Evidence shows that the Enneagram has been used by people across many cultures around the world for between 2,000 and 4,000 years.

The concept of the modern-day Enneagram is credited to Bolivian philosopher Oscar Ichazo, who in 1968 created the Arica Institute, a school that taught consciousness methodologies, including the Enneagram. Pioneering Chilean psychiatrist Claudio Naranjo came to Arica to learn more and instantly became interested in the Enneagram as a result of his own journey of self-discovery. He would go on to create the Seekers After Truth Institute, an international training program in which the Enneagram plays a central role.

The first books on the Enneagram weren't written until the 1980s. The popularity of the Enneagram died down in the 1990s and early 2000s; however, the past decade has seen renewed interest, perhaps due to information-sharing via the Internet. The concept of the Enneagram has grown and is now taught around the world at accredited schools operated through the International Enneagram Association. Psychologists and mental health therapists are beginning to use the Enneagram in their practices to help individuals recognize their motivations and how they may be holding them back.

BASICS OF THE ENNEAGRAM

The Enneagram is a tool to promote personal growth and self-development. It's a typing system (meaning it establishes "types") and a way to understand your motivations. Enneagram experts will be quick, however, to tell students that this methodology is not an excuse to engage in certain behaviors just because they may be typical of a certain type.

The Enneagram contains nine different types and nine ways of viewing the world. Enneagram theory maintains that everyone has a core fear and a core desire that make up their Enneagram type. This means that each person's core fear and core desire determine how they will act, respond, and interact with the world.

Enneagram educators and researchers agree that your Enneagram type is with you from a very young age, and it is not determined by the environment and world around you. The Enneagram is born of nature, not nurture. This means that you can have siblings who grow up in the same environment with similar experiences but completely different Enneagram types. Your type is determined by who you are, not what you've experienced. Through the Enneagram, you should be able to look back on your childhood and see how your motivations for doing certain things were always there. Of course, life experiences and trauma can come in and make things very confusing by causing you to react in uncharacteristic ways. Those trauma responses are called coping mechanisms and are not necessarily reflective of your motivations. Your Enneagram type cannot change, and it does not fluctuate depending on your season of life. What *will* change is how you interact with and use this information.

There are many titles and names for the nine types that are utilized across the Enneagram board. You will read more about the titles and types in chapter 2 after you take the self-assessment. The names that I use come from the Enneagram Institute, created in the 1990s by Don Richard Riso and Russ Hudson to research all the components of the Enneagram. Though the titles of each type give insight into the characteristics of that type, it's important to understand the depth of the Enneagram.

ENNEAGRAM STRUCTURE

At first glance, the Enneagram symbol can be confusing, both as to what it all means and how to interpret it. The word *Enneagram* stems from the Greek language, with *ennea* meaning "nine" and *gram* meaning "drawing" or "diagram." The Enneagram is a symbol made up of many different shapes and lines within the symbol itself. Let's explore what this means and some common terminology associated with the Enneagram.

Circle

The nine types, represented by corresponding numbers, are placed around a circle. This is intentional, representing the fact that all the Enneagram types are connected to each other. The circle is meant to represent unity and equality among the Enneagram types. We all come from the same place; we're all living in the same environment; we are all one and connected.

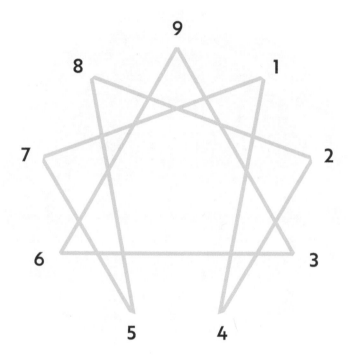

Numbers

The nine different numbers situated around the circle represent the personality types of the Enneagram. Each number represents a core fear, desire, and motivation for doing things, as well as stereotypical behaviors and ways of being and viewing the world. People tend to possess traits of all the types. However, we have the motivation of only one Enneagram personality; that is our type.

Triangle

In the middle of the Enneagram symbol is a perfect triangle, made up of types Three, Six, and Nine. This triangle functions as a middle ground for all the types, in addition to being representative of each of the Enneagram centers, or triads, which we'll explore in chapter 2. The points of the triangle serve as the middle ground for each of the centers as well.

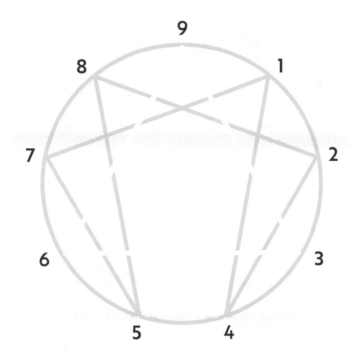

Hexad

This symbol connects the remaining types, indicating that they are also connected. This symbol also represents the fact that although our motivation will always remain in our main type, we often take on traits of other types, especially in times of growth or stress.

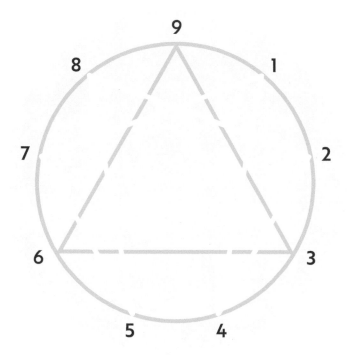

WINGS

Wings are the numbers on either side of your main Enneagram type. A common misconception is that a wing is just your second highest score when taking an Enneagram test. This could be the case, but only if it's a number that is next to your main type. You aren't just your main Enneagram type. You are also able to access the personality characteristics of your wings. The difference between your main type and the wings is that your main motivation will always lie in your Enneagram type. However, you may take on some of the behavior characteristics of your wings.

Most people have one wing that is stronger than the other. For example, I'm an Enneagram Two with a strong Three wing. However, that doesn't mean that I never access my One wing. It simply means that my Three wing is more developed. Some people feel like they don't relate to any characteristics of their wings. Part of understanding who you are overall is being able to incorporate characteristics from the wings into your main type.

The strength of your wings may change and fluctuate throughout your life. Your main Enneagram type will not change, but your main wing could go back and forth between the types on either side. You also may feel like you rely on one of your wings more during a specific period of your life, depending on life experiences or events.

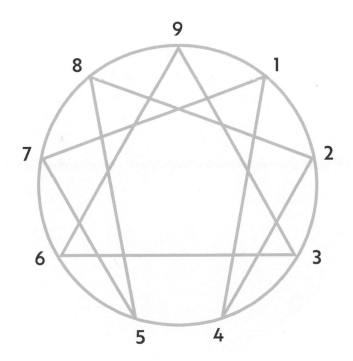

STRESS AND SECURITY POINTS

Each Enneagram type has two lines that point to specific directions on the Enneagram. The lines are actually arrows that lead to other Enneagram types, which are your type's stress point and security point.

The security point is the direction that your main Enneagram type moves to when you're in a healthy or secure time in your life. This is when true self-awareness and actualization occurs and you grow into the best version of yourself. This is where you want to be. People typically take on the healthy characteristics of their security point. For example, Enneagram Nine takes on healthy qualities of an Enneagram Three when they are feeling more secure. This can mean becoming more motivated and driven and feeling a desire to succeed.

The stress point is the direction that your main Enneagram type moves to when you're stressed out or in an unhealthy place. This can feel unfamiliar and foreign, as it's not your natural state of being and reacting. People typically take on the unhealthy characteristics of their stress point. Let's go back to the Enneagram Nine. When they are stressed, they take on unhealthy qualities of an Enneagram Six. This can mean experiencing more self-doubt, worry, and worst-case-scenario thinking. Having this knowledge and awareness of our propensities during such times can help prevent us from moving all the way down the stress line.

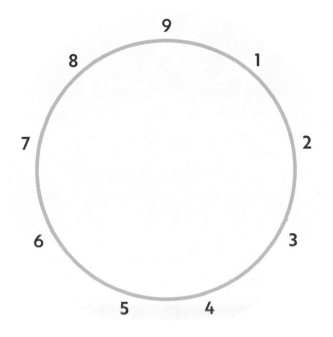

SECURITY POINTS

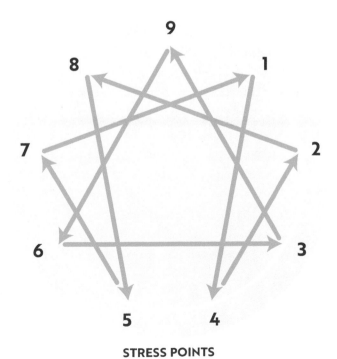

STRESS POINTS

LEVELS OF DEVELOPMENT

We've touched on a few healthy and unhealthy characteristics of Enneagram types. In fact, every Enneagram type has three levels of development: healthy, average, and unhealthy. These levels relate to where we are as far as our overall sense of emotional wellness, and they typically coincide with healthy and unhealthy behaviors.

It's important to remember that your Enneagram type is determined by what motivates you to do the things that you do. The levels of development consist of specific behaviors that correspond to each type. When an Enneagram type is in a good place, they are considered "healthy." When healthy, the person feels like they are free to express themselves through wide ranges of behavior. Most people fall under the "average" level of development, which is when we are in a neutral place. Here we focus more on our identity and the way that others are viewing us. When we're not at our best, we are in the "unhealthy" level of development. During these times, we tend to see ourselves differently than how others see us. We are not in tune with our identity at all.

Healthy versus unhealthy behaviors are different from the behaviors associated with the stress versus security lines. When I refer to the stress line, these are behaviors that Enneagram types tend to take on when they are experiencing periods of stress. For example, an Enneagram Two might snap into being aggressive, which is more characteristic of an Enneagram Eight. They might be considered a "healthy" Two, but this one stressful moment led them to access their stress line. Security appears differently and it is also situational, like when we are having a moment or experience in a good place or feeling secure in who we are. We can be a healthy version of our type, while not being in security or growth.

CHAPTER 2

Discover Your Enneagram

THE ENNEAGRAM TEST

There are many Enneagram tests available to help you determine your main type. Some tests even provide you with your stronger Enneagram wing as well. Many Enneagram tests are very good at assessing behaviors; however, we know that the Enneagram is based on motivations, not behaviors. Additionally, as mentioned in chapter 1, we often answer questions to match the ways we want other people to perceive us. The best way to figure out your Enneagram type is to look at the core fears and motivations of each type and see what resonates with you, so although tests are a great place to start, it's just the beginning of truly discovering who you are and who you can be.

SELF-ASSESSING YOUR ENNEAGRAM TYPE

Let's begin your journey with a self-assessment. Although this is not an "official" Enneagram test, it should give you an excellent starting point for recognizing the motivations that most closely align for you.

Begin by reading all the possible types. Each type has three statements that you can check off to keep track of the traits that resonate most with you. As you go through each type, be thoughtful about the process and keep an open mind. Don't just think about your life currently; reflect on your childhood and your life as a whole. Remember that even if you've experienced traumatic events or life situations, your motivations for doing things should have remained the same as they were throughout the whole of your life. To perform an accurate assessment, really think about why you do the things you do—these are the motivations behind your behaviors and actions. Be cautious of choosing a possibility just because you want to be that person. Be as honest with yourself as possible.

After you have read through each type, see which types you checked off the most. If you have several, keep working through them to choose one that you most connect with. This will be your type.

TYPE ONE:

Ethical and conscientious, you tend to feel a strong need to improve yourself and others. You have a set of ideals and values that are important to you, and you want people to do the right thing. You're known for being organized and creating order, and you maintain high standards for yourself and others. You might have problems with resentment and being critical of others if they do things differently than you. At your best, you are inspiring, wise, and principled. You want to be good, have integrity, and be balanced. Fairness is important to you. You fear being seen as a bad person, corrupt, or wrong.

- ☐ Dissatisfied with the status quo, you feel that it is up to you to improve everything.

- ☐ Afraid of making a mistake, you desire for everything to be consistent with your ideals.

- ☐ You are impatient and never satisfied unless things are done "properly."

TYPE TWO:

Warmhearted and focused on relationships, you tend to discount your own needs and feelings to serve others. You want people to feel loved and wanted, and you might have problems with people-pleasing and trouble saying "no." At your best, you are patient, altruistic, and forgiving. You want to be loved, wanted, needed, and appreciated for your good deeds and what you do for others. You fear being unworthy of love and care from others. You strive to improve others' lives by always being there for them. It's important to you to be liked and accepted by others, but also to alleviate the world of its problems.

- ☐ Helping others gives you a sense of purpose.

- ☐ You feel like you instinctively know what other people need from you and how they are feeling.

- ☐ You wish people knew what you needed instead of you having to tell them because you feel like it would show that they care.

TYPE THREE:

Ambitious and focused on results, you tend to encourage others to be the best that they can be. You might have problems with being too focused on appearances or adjusting who you are depending on who is around you at the time. At your best, you are competent, enthusiastic, and accomplished. You want to be accepted, valued, successful, and respected for the work that you do. You fear failure and feeling worthless. You often think that you are what you do. You strive to be celebrated for your achievements and you want to celebrate others, as well. It's important to you to be the best at what you do and to be accepted for who you are.

- ☐ You want to be celebrated for your achievements.

- ☐ You tend to put aside emotions because they can get in the way of what you want to accomplish.

- ☐ You tend to overwork and become at risk for burnout.

TYPE FOUR:

Creative and focused on aesthetics, you tend to encourage authenticity and self-expression, both physically and emotionally. You might have problems with comparing yourself to others, extreme sensitivity to criticism, and being seen as self-absorbed. At your best, you are empathetic, caring, and highly intuitive to others' feelings. You want to make a significant impact and to have a unique identity that allows you to truly feel like yourself. You fear being seen as defective, like something is wrong with you, or having no identity at all. You strive to always see the beauty in everything and to only have deep and meaningful connections with others. It's important to you to truly be seen, heard, and understood.

☐ You enjoy sitting with your sadness and don't always want to be cheered up.

☐ You constantly look for deep connections and meaningful experiences.

☐ You often compare yourself and what you have (or don't have) to others.

TYPE FIVE:

Independent and focused on intellect, you tend to learn everything there is to know about a topic. You may find that you spend more time observing life than fully participating in it. You might have problems with being seen as arrogant, withdrawn, or stingy with your time and resources. At your best, you are dependable, understanding, and objective. You are a great sounding board for others and truly self-sufficient. You want to be knowledgeable and competent. You fear being incapable of doing something and having your energy depleted. You strive to always understand the world and everyone in it. It's important to you for people to respect and honor your boundaries.

- [ ] You feel more energized when you spend time by yourself.

- [ ] When you're interested in something, you want to know everything about that topic.

- [ ] You stand back and observe, often finding that more comfortable than participating in activities.

TYPE SIX:

Community-oriented and focused on stability, you tend to always be prepared and think things through. You might have problems with worst-case-scenario thinking, anxiety, or pessimism. At your best, you are courageous and responsible with a strong sense of humor. You want to have support, guidance, and security from the people and environment around you. You typically fear fear itself, but also that you will be left alone without support, guidance, or security. You strive to always have a plan for what could happen and be prepared for whatever comes your way. It's important to you to have commitment from others.

- [ ] You often think about what could go wrong and plan accordingly.

- [ ] You have a difficult time trusting others, even though trust is very important to you.

- [ ] You experience self-doubt and second-guess your decisions and actions often.

TYPE SEVEN:

Flexible and focused on having fun, you tend to view the world as an opportunity to experience new things and adventures. You might have problems with being impatient, impulsive, and unable to focus at times. At your best, you are creative, practical, and adventurous. You want freedom, but you are ultimately searching for contentment. You fear missing out on things, but you are mostly afraid of being trapped in emotional pain or having to deal with negativity. You strive to never be constrained and to maintain your independence. It's important to you to create meaningful relationships with others and to always be optimistic.

- ☐ You often see the world through rose-colored glasses.

- ☐ People come to you to be cheered up or to help them look on the bright side.

- ☐ You have an inability to sit still because you always want to move on to the next thing.

TYPE EIGHT:

Decisive and focused on protecting yourself and others, you tend to stand up for others and cheer on the underdog. You might have problems with being quick to anger, confrontational, and domineering. At your best, you are influential, decisive, and passionate. You are also very honest, even when the truth hurts. You want to be able to control your situation and environment and determine next steps yourself. You fear being seen as weak or being controlled or harmed by others. You strive to avoid vulnerability because that can be perceived as weakness. It's important to you to fight for injustices and to protect the vulnerable.

- ☐ You have an ability to quickly make decisions without much thought.

- ☐ You feel comfortable debating and dealing with conflict.

- ☐ You wish other people could stand up for themselves like you do.

TYPE NINE:

Patient and focused on making sure everyone else is okay, you tend to go with the flow and offer nonjudgmental perspectives. You might have problems with decision-making, not speaking up when you have a thought or opinion, or becoming passive-aggressive. At your best, you are kind, generous, and open with your feelings. You want to maintain your inner peace and stability.

You fear conflict the most, but this is because you're afraid of losing or being abandoned by the people who are close to you. You strive to see all sides of a situation and to be open and accepting of everyone. It's important to you to take the time to relax and focus on cultivating important relationships.

- ☐ You typically let other people decide what they want to do or where they want to go.

- ☐ You often wish that you could escape to a more peaceful place or reality.

- ☐ People often view you as a nonjudgmental and accepting person.

The Nine Types

Now that you have narrowed down the possibilities, read the following to see if you can discover which type you are. The order of the Enneagram types below corresponds to the order of possible types you read about in the self-assessment section above.

ENNEAGRAM ONE—THE REFORMER: Focused on being ethical and right, they make sure that they are seen as a good person and that they are doing the right thing. They have a strong sense of right versus wrong, and they want to make the world a better place. They are responsible, organized, and conscientious. They might be teachers, journalists, or at any job that focuses on justice.

ENNEAGRAM TWO—THE HELPER: Their focus lies in meeting others' needs by being caring and generous with their time and resources. They are empathetic, with an ability to know what other people need and how they are feeling. They might be a counselor or social worker focused on helping others.

ENNEAGRAM THREE—THE ACHIEVER: Focused on success, they enjoy being valuable and able to get the job done. They are motivated, optimistic, hardworking, and goal-oriented. They might be an entrepreneur, business person, or other professional focused on actively trying to climb the ladder.

ENNEAGRAM FOUR—THE INDIVIDUALIST: Their focus lies in maintaining their individuality and presenting themselves in an authentic and transparent way. They are self-aware, expressive, romantic, and true to themselves. They might be a designer, artist, or creator focused on creating significant experiences.

ENNEAGRAM FIVE—THE INVESTIGATOR: They are focused on gaining an understanding of things and providing insight to others. They are knowledgeable, innovative, and extremely private. They might be a researcher, actuary, or professional focused on mastering a specific trade or specialty.

ENNEAGRAM SIX—THE LOYALIST: Focused on security, they desire to maintain a level of comfort that feels right to them. They are reliable, trustworthy, devoted, and committed to everything around them. They might be a project manager, teacher, or journalist focused on organization and passionate about a cause.

ENNEAGRAM SEVEN—THE ENTHUSIAST: Their focus lies in experiencing as many things as they can and living life to the fullest. They are energetic, enthusiastic, joyful, and optimistic. They might be a publicist, entrepreneur, or anything that has to do with travel and will probably be focused on entertainment and not sitting still.

ENNEAGRAM EIGHT—THE CHALLENGER: They are focused on protecting themselves and others and on being a strong person. They are honest, assertive, independent, and happy to take charge. They might be a sales director, activist, or at any job that is focused on and always working toward leadership.

ENNEAGRAM NINE—THE PEACEMAKER: Their focus lies in maintaining a peaceful environment for themselves and the people around them. They are easygoing, adaptable, understanding, and supportive. They might be a counselor, human resources manager, or mediator focused on resolving situations.

THREE CENTERS

There are three different centers, also known as triads, that make up the Enneagram: the gut center (instinctual center), heart center (feeling center), and head center (thinking center). The centers help describe the way we interact with the world, and they ultimately explain where our decision-making process begins. Each center contains three Enneagram types, and those types share similar processes, perceptions, and feelings. Your main Enneagram type will determine which center you fall in. You could very well exhibit the traits from other centers, but your main center in which you fall will be your natural way of being and interacting.

→ The gut center Enneagram types receive information through their gut or body and then instinctively respond when making a decision or reacting.

→ The heart center Enneagram types receive information through their heart and then rely on their emotions or feelings before responding.

→ The head center Enneagram types receive information through their head and then think things through before responding.

Each center/triad also houses a specific dominant emotion:

→ The gut center experiences anger more than the other centers; it simply appears differently for the types in this center.

→ The dominant emotion for the heart center is shame. Twos avoid shame by making sure they are doing enough to help those around them.

→ The types in the head center relate to the dominant emotion of fear, but all three types fear different things.

THE GUT CENTER
9

8   1

7   2

THE HEAD CENTER

6   3

THE HEART CENTER

5   4

By identifying how you respond to information, how you make decisions, and your dominant emotion, you can further narrow down what your Enneagram type may be.

The Gut Center

The gut center contains Enneagram types Eight, Nine, and One. These types share the characteristics that make up the gut center. The gut center is also referred to as the instinctive center. This is because the Enneagram types in this center tend to focus on taking action first and thinking or considering feelings later. The types in this center generally "trust their gut" to lead them in the right direction, causing them to make decisions quickly. Enneagram types Eight and One rely on their gut to be quick with their decision-making. Enneagram Nines also trust their gut, but it often leads to indecisiveness. The Enneagram types in this center have a hard time understanding how an individual's emotions could get in the way of logic and understanding.

Those in the gut center tend to struggle with anger. Anger comes naturally for Enneagram Eights, and they express it without any filter. Enneagram Nines tend to bury angry feelings, pretending they don't exist, only to have them expressed in a passive-aggressive way. Enneagram Ones feel that it's inappropriate to be angry and typically describe it as "annoyance" or "frustration" instead.

The Heart Center

The heart center contains Enneagram types Two, Three, and Four. All of these types share specific characteristics related to the heart or feeling. These Enneagram types receive information through their heart and consider how they feel about things before they respond or make decisions. The Enneagram types in the heart center are more in tune with their emotions than others. They use their feelings and emotions to figure out how they relate to the world around them and what needs to be done.

The Enneagram types in the heart center all have a relationship with shame. Enneagram Twos typically feel shame around whether they're doing enough for other people. For Enneagram Threes, their shame is focused on whether they are achieving enough. Enneagram Fours typically struggle with feelings surrounding whether they are enough in general. All the types in the heart triad are seeking significance and meaning from experiences. They have a hard time understanding those who aren't emotional and in tune with their feelings or those who just instinctively act without seeing how they feel about it first. They may also get frustrated with those who spend so much time thinking about things that they miss the experiences in front of them.

The Head Center

The head center contains Enneagram types Five, Six, and Seven. These types share specific characteristics that are related to the head or thinking. Each of these Enneagram types receive information through their head and spend time thinking about it before responding. These Enneagram types typically spend more time in their heads than other Enneagram types. They think things through, process what is going on, and anticipate what could happen.

The types in the head center typically have a relationship with anxiety. They don't necessarily think of it as experiencing anxiety, just that they are planning and preparing. Enneagram Fives feel anxiety because of their fear of depletion of their resources. Enneagram Sixes often experience anxiety because of their need to anticipate every scenario. For Enneagram Sevens, the tendency is to bury the anxiety and act like it doesn't exist. All the types in the head center seek security, and they rely on their head to make decisions. They have a hard time understanding how people don't spend time thinking or processing information before making decisions. They also don't understand how people can trust their emotions and feelings more than their head.

PART II

Every Enneagram

I n this part, we will delve more deeply into each Enneagram type. We'll discuss their typical behaviors, what motivates those behaviors, and how each type relates to others in familial, work, and romantic relationships, and with friends. We will also look at how and when each type is likely to flourish or struggle.

The behaviors discussed for each type are stereotypical behaviors, or the most common behaviors that each type express as they act on their motivations. It is important to note that these descriptions are not blanket descriptions. Each person will act based on their unique history, context, and relationships with other people. The goal is not to put people in boxes, but to provide a broad understanding of the connection between motivation, behaviors, and relationships.

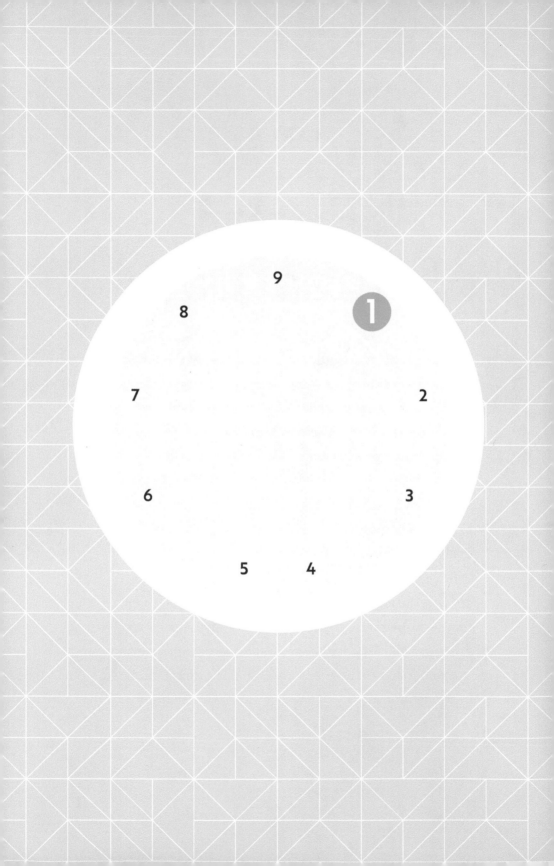

The Reformer

HOW REFORMERS ACT

Enneagram Ones, or Reformers, are known for their strong sense of right and wrong and their constant quest to be as ethical and moral as possible. It's very important for them to follow rules, but only if the rules make sense to them. It's almost more about making sure they are doing the right thing. They are known for their attention to detail and organization because that feels like the "right" thing for them to do. They have high standards and expectations for themselves and others because they believe that others should also be focused on doing the right thing.

MOTIVATIONS

Enneagram Ones are motivated by a desire to be good, ethical, moral, and right. They want to be seen as a good person, and they want to make a difference in the world. Because their biggest desire is to be a good person, their behaviors reflect that by valuing fairness and honesty. Ones are also motivated by the fear of being bad, corrupt, or immoral. They want to make sure that other people do not see them as a bad person. They also try to make sure they are always "right," whether that means knowing the right thing to do, the right answer, or the right thing to say. They are also motivated by their fear of being wrong, and they may have a hard time admitting when they are.

STRESS AND SECURITY POINTS

The Enneagram symbol shows the other numbers that each Enneagram type is connected to. These points are often referred to as stress and security points because we often go to these types in times of stress or security. Even though we can take on all aspects of the types that we're connected to, we typically exhibit the negative qualities of our stress point and the positive qualities of our security point. For Enneagram Ones, the stress point is Four, the Individualist, and the security point is Seven, the Enthusiast.

Ones typically become stressed out when they don't live up to their own expectations, when they feel like they are the only responsible people, and when they are losing control over a situation. When stressed, Ones will exhibit some of the negative aspects of a Four. This can look like withdrawing and becoming consumed with their emotions. They can also start to feel like no one understands them or what they are experiencing.

When in a state of growth or security, Ones take on the positive qualities of a Seven. The stereotypically rigid One will feel more adventurous and carefree. They will not be so concerned about making mistakes and will adopt a "glass half-full" mentality.

WINGS

Because wings are located on either side of your main type, Enneagram One's wings are Nine, the Peacemaker, and Two, the Helper. Most people have one wing that is stronger than the other.

A One with a stronger Nine wing is also called the Idealist. They are typically more focused on keeping the peace. They may be more gentle and soft-spoken and not as opinionated as a typical One might be. They also tend to care less about what others think of them than a One with a Two wing. This is because the One with the Nine wing is less in tune with their emotions. A One with a Nine wing may avoid conflict and confrontation more than the typical One.

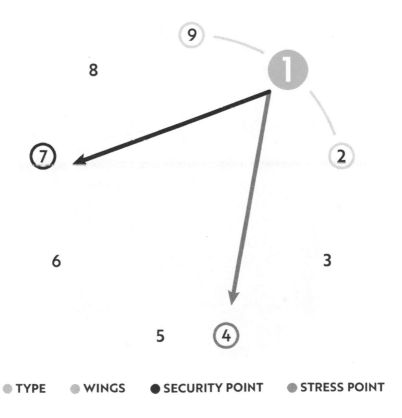

● TYPE   ● WINGS   ● SECURITY POINT   ● STRESS POINT

A One with a Two wing is also called the Advocate. They are more focused on relationships and meeting others' needs; thus they are more outspoken and social than other Ones. A One with a Two wing is also more critical of themselves and might feel like they need to strive more to be seen as a good person because of a Two's connection to shame. Ones with a Two wing are more likely to be able to see a problem and fix it.

WHAT'S EASY FOR REFORMERS

Because of their desire to do things well, Reformers can typically focus on getting the job done and work hard to accomplish whatever goal they set for themselves. The ability to structure, create a plan, and pay attention to details typically comes easily to them because those abilities often lead to completion of goals. Ones are also good at making sure they don't compromise themselves for other people. They have high standards and expectations and will make those expectations known to other people. Ones are naturally able to create order out of chaos and organization out of a disaster.

WHAT'S HARD FOR REFORMERS

Enneagram Ones struggle with being critical of themselves and others. Every Enneagram One that I talk to says that they have an inner critic telling them that they need to be better, do better, and improve themselves in some way. Ones are often very surprised to find out that other types don't have this same inner critic. Because they are often critical of others, Ones feel like they are the only ones who can do something the "right" way. Because of this, people may be afraid to help them with something, which in turn perpetuates the cycle of Ones feeling like everything falls on them and leaving them feeling overwhelmed.

HEALTHY BEHAVIORS

Ones' focus on doing the right thing tends to lead to behaviors that encourage fairness, order, and productivity. That focus also makes Ones act responsibly and encourage responsibility in others. When they are in a good emotional place, Ones let go of the need for perfection and accept life as it comes. They forgive themselves and others. As they do, they inspire others to be the best that they can be, knowing that perfection isn't attainable. They relinquish control and trust the process without being so hard on themselves and others.

UNHEALTHY BEHAVIORS

Enneagram Ones can tend to be overly critical and judgmental, not just about others, but also about themselves. They can be so focused on mistakes that they are unable to see past them. They feel like they need to strive for perfection and be something that is ultimately unattainable. Ones can get stuck in ruts when they become fixated on "shoulds": They "should" do this, they "should" be better, I "should not" have done that. Some Ones may micromanage themselves and others, feeling the need to maintain control.

WORK LIFE

Enneagram Ones are responsible, hardworking, and honest. Like in other areas of their life, they have high standards and expectations for themselves and others in the workplace. Group projects can be difficult for Ones because they often feel like they are the only ones responsible enough to get the job done or the only ones who can do things the "correct" way. Ones will work on a project until it is exactly the way they want it. They don't take shortcuts to get the job done quicker because they don't want to make a mistake. They will do whatever they have to do to deliver the type of work they would expect from others. When working with a One, be mindful of the amount of work on their plate and offer to assist them. They may turn you down, but reminding Ones that there are others willing to help and take on responsibility may help them feel more secure.

FAMILY LIFE

Enneagram Ones are often the glue that holds a family unit together. This is because of their ability to create order, keep everyone and everything organized, and maintain structure. Ones typically value family life and the connections within the family unit, but they may feel overwhelmed taking on the responsibility of cultivating family relationships. As parents, Ones take on the responsibility of teaching their children right from wrong and how to be responsible humans. As siblings, Ones are typically the leaders who like to call the shots and be in charge. Their siblings or family peers typically look up to them as their moral compass. Ones may get frustrated with family members who don't value the same things that they do and express their criticism more freely because of their close familial relationship. If you have a family member who is a One, encourage them to do things that they enjoy doing instead of activities that they feel like they "should" be engaging in.

RELATIONSHIP LIFE

Enneagram Ones are usually attracted to people who share the same values, morals, and beliefs because of how important those qualities are to them. They will not compromise their beliefs to make someone else feel comfortable. Ones need to be careful of their expectations of partners and friends because of the resentment that could arise if their loved ones don't meet those expectations. Ones make great romantic partners because of their willingness to fight for what they believe in, their dedication to the relationship, and their need for truth and honesty.

In friendships, you'll always know where you stand with a One. They are consistent, dependable, and intentional about the time they spend with you. They are always there and willing to help. However, Ones need to be mindful of unintentionally judging their friends for doing things differently. Conversely, friends of Ones need to remind them that they are perfect the way they are.

REFORMERS AND OTHER ENNEAGRAM TYPES

One of the most popular questions I get is, "What type would I get along with the best?" We all have different strengths and areas for growth when it comes to our interactions with other Enneagram types. Enneagram Ones tend to get along well with other Enneagram types because of their decisiveness and attention to detail. This can balance out some of the relationships. Here are some dynamics you might see in relationships with a One.

WITH ONES:
Ones can get along really well with other Ones because they can truly understand where the other person is coming from. They share common ground regarding the importance of values, morals, and ethics, and they enjoy planning and having a routine. However, they may struggle with high expectations of one another.

WITH TWOS:
Twos get along well with Ones because they have a shared value of relationships and connection. However, Twos can sometimes feel resentful if their needs aren't getting met by Ones.

WITH THREES:

Threes and Ones can look similar because of their shared ability to get things done and drive to succeed. However, they may both bury emotions and feelings, resulting in situations where nothing gets resolved.

WITH FOURS:

Ones and Fours can understand each other at times because they are connected on the Enneagram—Ones turn to Four behaviors when they are stressed. They both value self-improvement and making a difference. However, Fours are very sensitive to criticism and may take offense at a One's honesty.

WITH FIVES:

Ones and Fives get along well because they both excel at setting and respecting boundaries. However, they can both be judgmental at times and can neglect their own emotions.

WITH SIXES:

Ones and Sixes tend to understand each other because they are both loyal and committed and they have strong values and beliefs. They may struggle because they both place a lot of responsibility on themselves and have a difficult time if things don't go their way.

WITH SEVENS:

Ones and Sevens are also connected on the Enneagram, so they share a unique understanding. Remember, Ones turn to Seven behaviors when they feel secure. Sevens help Ones be more carefree, whereas Ones help Sevens be more organized. They may get impatient with each other because they often value different things.

WITH EIGHTS:

Ones and Eights look similar because both can be opinionated and strong-willed. They get along well when they understand each other's protectiveness and passion for justice. However, power struggles may occur, especially when both want to be in charge.

WITH NINES:

Ones and Nines both value comfort and daily routines. They like to participate in what is familiar to them. This combination can conflict at times if Ones are too critical of Nines. Nines avoid conflict at all costs, and Ones don't typically shy away from it.

Reformer Mantras

When things get tough or whenever you feel like it, repeat these mantras and affirmations out loud or in your head to help center yourself. You can repeat one or say them one after another.

I am good.

I am okay even when
I make mistakes.

I am perfect just the
way I am.

Judging others is not
my responsibility.

I can let go of what
I cannot change.

REFORMER EXERCISE

The goal of this exercise is to work on silencing your inner critic. When your inner critic is loud, it's difficult to focus on your strengths or accept all the positive things about yourself.

1. Whenever you experience a negative thought about yourself, replace it with a positive one. For example, instead of, *I should have gotten more done today*, think, *I was able to get this done today*. This will help you shift from your perceived faults and failures to your accomplishments and open yourself up to positive feelings and confidence.

2. Practice this shift by creating a two-column list: On one side, write down the critical thoughts, then cross them out and rewrite them as positive thoughts in the other column.

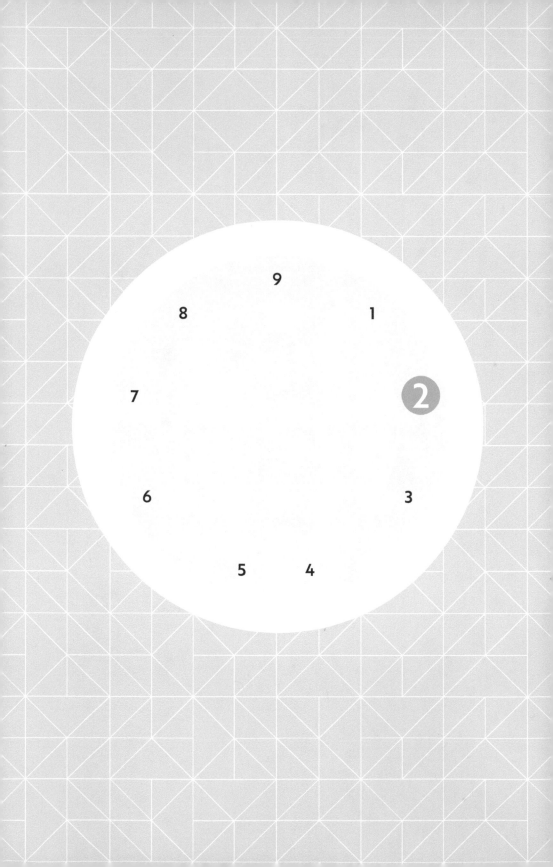

TYPE 2

The Helper

HOW HELPERS ACT

Enneagram Twos, the Helpers, have also been called the Givers, the Companions, and the Supportive Advisors. All these names mean the same thing: These people are supportive and helpful to the people around them. Helpers want other people to feel loved and wanted, and they want to be the person who makes them feel that way. They are focused on relationships and serving others, but sometimes they discount what they need from other people. They want to be needed, but oftentimes end up neglecting their own needs at the same time. Twos feel like it is their life's purpose to make a difference in others' lives, and they do so by assessing and fulfilling whatever is needed in that moment.

MOTIVATIONS

Enneagram Twos are motivated by a need to feel loved, wanted, and appreciated by others. They often do things to make other people feel loved and wanted because they want to feel that in return. Because they also want to be needed by others, they make themselves indispensable to the people around them. They make sure they have something that other people need from them. Twos are also motivated by their biggest fear: not being loved, wanted, or even liked by others. This is why some of the behaviors of Helpers involve doing whatever they can to stay in the good graces of the people closest to them.

Famous Helpers

Though we don't know what motivates other people, these are observational assessments. Let these guesses help you determine your own type.

Mary Kay Ash	"Rubeus Hagrid"
Maya Angelou	Eleanor Roosevelt
Lionel Richie	Mother Teresa

They sometimes subconsciously do things for others for the appreciation and approval they will receive from it.

STRESS AND SECURITY POINTS

Enneagram Twos' security point is Four, the Individualist, and their stress point is Eight, the Challenger. When secure, Twos will take on positive characteristics of a Four. When stressed, they will take on some negative qualities of an Eight. Let's talk about what that could look like.

When a Two is in growth, they can take on Fours' positive attributes and are honest about their motivations for doing things. This allows them to be more in tune with their own emotions and feelings and understand when their needs are not being met. Twos in growth will also be able to accept painful feelings and emotions as part of their reality. They will no longer try to mask those feelings by doing things for others.

When a Two isn't in a good place, they often feel like they are losing control. They may take on Eights' negative attributes, becoming sharper with their tone and more aggressive toward others. When overwhelmed, Twos will feel like they want to withdraw their support and care for others because it is not deserved. They can demand a lot from others.

WINGS

An Enneagram Two has a One (the Reformer) wing and a Three (the Achiever) wing. Although your motivations will always lie in your main Enneagram type, you could take on personality characteristics of your wings. It might seem like a Two with a One wing and a Two with a Three wing would look similar, but they are actually quite different.

A Two with a One wing is also referred to as the Servant. They are typically more focused on self-control, and they are more organized and very aware of what is right and wrong in the world. A Two with a One wing will also feel more responsibility when it comes to helping others. They feel like it is their duty to make things right in the world by being generous and helpful.

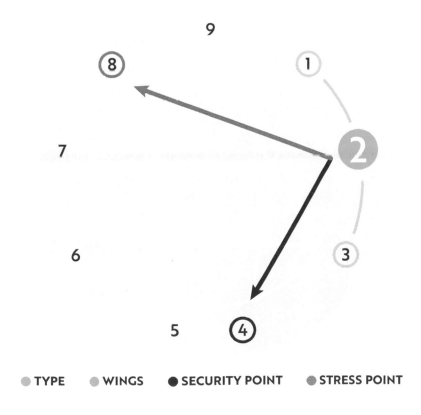

● TYPE　　● WINGS　　● SECURITY POINT　　● STRESS POINT

A Two with a Three wing is also called the Host/Hostess. They are more social and outgoing than other Twos. They care more about their reputation and being celebrated for their achievements and successes. They are personable and able to talk to anyone in a room full of people. A Two with a Three wing cares more about being liked and valued for what they bring to a relationship.

WHAT'S EASY FOR HELPERS

Helpers are naturally able to read a room and determine what other people are feeling and what they need. It's also very easy for Twos to be empathetic. Twos know what other people need and how to fulfill that need. Because Helpers are so relationship-oriented, they naturally relate to and offer a sense of understanding to the people around them. They make others feel welcome and wanted because they want other people to do the same for them. They are really good at making other people feel loved.

WHAT'S HARD FOR HELPERS

Because of their need to please others, it can be extremely difficult for Twos to say "no." They feel that if they say "no," people will think differently about them. Twos also tend to struggle with identifying and communicating what they need and desire. This is because they are more comfortable addressing what *other* people need. Any sort of criticism is also difficult for Twos, as it threatens their security of feeling loved and wanted by others. I always say that if you're trying to offer constructive criticism to a Two, stick with the sandwich method: Begin with a compliment, insert the criticism, and follow up with another compliment.

HEALTHY BEHAVIORS

An Enneagram Two is kind, empathetic, and giving of their time, energy, and resources. Growth occurs for Twos when they are selfless and willing to put others before themselves. Twos are typically helpful in all circumstances; however, sometimes their help has strings attached. When able to focus on the helpful act itself, as opposed to how someone will view them afterward, they can grow from the act of giving from a true place where they expect nothing in return. A Two's ability to be confident in who they are and what they have to offer will allow them to only engage in the things that they want to do, instead of feeling like they have to say "yes" to everything and everyone. Twos are then able to acknowledge their own needs and communicate that to the people in their lives.

UNHEALTHY BEHAVIORS

When Enneagram Twos only focus on feeling needed, they are more self-focused with their giving; that is, they tend to do things for others to see what they receive in return. They can become resentful if they don't receive appreciation and may start to keep track of the things they have done for other people. Because they want to be liked, they say "yes" to everything to ensure that they are pleasing others. They may also insert themselves where they aren't needed, just to make other people need them. When Twos are not as confident in addressing and identifying their own needs, they can be very dependent on others and not able to stand on their own. They tend to neglect the fact that they have needs of their own and think that other people will just be able to read their mind. This leads to immense frustration, and they may begin to feel like they are the only ones who do things for others. They may become so focused on not being left out that they do whatever they can to make sure that doesn't happen.

WORK LIFE

Enneagram Twos in the workplace are extremely people-oriented and focused on their relationships in the workplace. They are typically always there to support their coworkers, inside and outside of the workplace environment. They walk into a room and naturally know how other people are feeling and what they need, which helps them easily find friends in the workplace. They are genuinely surprised when people don't like them or care for their personality. They always ask what they can do to help and how they can fulfill others' needs. However, Twos can struggle with personal boundaries, as they may not be able to separate personal life from professional life, leading to those lines getting crossed. They want to share their personal life with their coworkers because they want to hear about others' lives. If you work with a Two, appreciate the things they do to help you and be gentle with criticism.

FAMILY LIFE

Like in other areas of their lives, Enneagram Twos are supportive, caring, and attentive to their family members. They love to encourage their family members and want to make sure they feel loved and wanted throughout their lives. From knowing what a family member wants for their birthday to daily words of encouragement, Twos always show up. Even though a family's love is unconditional, Twos still feel like they have to do things for their relatives to feel loved. They may worry that they aren't doing enough for their family, which can lead to additional efforts to please their family members. As children, Twos just want to please their parents and feel loved and wanted by them. As parents, Twos are loving and supportive of everything their children do. It is important to Twos that their family members show them they love them.

RELATIONSHIP LIFE

Enneagram Twos view relationships as the most important thing in their lives. They often look to others for warmth, emotional connection, and understanding because they know that they offer these characteristics to others. However, Twos need to be careful not to give too much of themselves in relationships. Although they are really good at making their partners feel loved and supported in all their endeavors, they are less likely to communicate their own needs and desires to their partner because they are not used to other people taking care of them. In relationships, Twos often fear rejection. They struggle with feeling good enough and worthy enough to be in the relationship. This can lead to burnout and a sense that their actions are not being reciprocated. If you're in a relationship with a Two, it's important to be specific and detailed when communicating what you like about them. Words are important to Enneagram Twos.

HELPERS AND OTHER ENNEAGRAM TYPES

Enneagram Twos generally get along well with other people because of their ability to understand others. Here are some dynamics you might see in relationships with an Enneagram Two.

WITH ONES:
Twos and Ones get along well because they both are service-oriented. Both types enjoy being needed and doing things for others.

WITH TWOS:
Twos can understand each other especially well because they have shared motivations and reasons for doing things. They understand each other's need to feel loved and wanted and can often deliver on that.

WITH THREES:

Twos and Threes share encouraging and motivational qualities. They also both care a great deal about others' opinions of them.

WITH FOURS:

Twos and Fours are connected on the Enneagram, and both tend to be emotional and in tune with their feelings. They can sometimes be overly dramatic.

WITH FIVES:

Twos and Fives struggle to understand each other at times because Twos are emotional and Fives tend to avoid feelings. However, they can really balance each other out because of this.

WITH SIXES:

Twos and Sixes share a need for connection and relationship. They both value loyalty and honesty. However, they may both struggle with a fear of abandonment.

WITH SEVENS:

Twos and Sevens are both optimistic and full of life. They also deeply value the people in their lives. However, Twos are not as spontaneous as Sevens.

WITH EIGHTS:

Twos and Eights have an interesting dynamic, one that ends up being strong. They are connected on the Enneagram in that Twos go to Eight in times of stress and Eights go to Two in times of growth. They may seem like opposites with their behaviors, but because of this, they are able to understand where the other person is coming from. They both have a passion for helping others.

WITH NINES:

Twos and Nines sometimes look similar, but Twos are more proactive with their helping, whereas Nines react to a need or call for help. However, they are both empathetic, kind, and caring.

Helper Mantras

When things get tough or whenever you feel like it, repeat these mantras and affirmations out loud or in your head to help center yourself. You can repeat one or say them one after another.

I am wanted and loved.

I am appreciated for what I contribute.

My needs are important.

I can love without expectations.

I can say "no" without feeling guilty.

HELPER EXERCISE

The goal of this exercise is to truly understand why you are doing something for another person and assess if it's something you really want to do or something you're doing out of obligation. By understanding the motivations behind your giving, you can avoid resentment caused by unmet expectations. You can also strengthen your ability to recognize and address your own needs. Let's talk about how to do this.

1. When you wake up in the morning, write down what you need for that day. At the end of the day, review the list to check off which needs were met. Do this for one week.

2. After one week, write down all the things that you did for others that week. Why did you want to do those things for others? What were you expecting in return? Did you truly enjoy doing it?

9

8   1

7   2

                    3

6

5   4

The Achiever

HOW ACHIEVERS ACT

Enneagram Threes are called the Achievers because that is one of their main goals in life. Achievers are driven, motivated, and focused on being successful and the best that they can be. Focused on the end result, they typically don't stop working until the job is done. Achievers are naturally competitive because of their need to be the best, and they will often encourage others to be their very best as well. Threes have a chameleon-like ability to adjust who they are based on who they are around. They know what they have to do to be liked and respected by others. Appearances are extremely important to Achievers.

MOTIVATIONS

Enneagram Threes are motivated by a need to be valued and respected. They believe that if they work hard enough, other people will respect them and what they have to offer. They also want to be seen as competent, and they want people to come to them to get the job done. Achievers fear failure the most, but they also fear being seen as incapable or unable to do something. Because of this, they work to make sure they are always able to complete the task. Threes are motivated to set goals for themselves and know that they will meet them.

Famous Achievers

Though we don't know what motivates other people, these are observational assessments. Let these guesses help you determine your own type.

Muhammad Ali	Dwayne Johnson
"Leslie Knope"	Taylor Swift
Arnold Schwarzenegger	Oprah Winfrey

STRESS AND SECURITY POINTS

When in a secure place, Enneagram Threes will take on some of the healthy qualities of a Six, the Loyalist. When stressed, Threes will take on unhealthy traits of Nine, the Peacemaker. Each of these types can show up in the Achiever in many ways.

When a Three is secure, they take on the Six's abilities to slow down and recognize that they aren't defined by their achievements. They tend to encourage others more and find increased value in their relationships with others. This looks like being more loyal, a team player, and less competitive. When healthy, Threes will also help themselves and others prepare for whatever comes their way.

When a Three is in a state of stress, they will adopt unhealthy traits of a Nine, such as losing motivation and becoming overwhelmed at everything that needs to be done. They also can become withdrawn, socially removed, and passive aggressive. When stressed, Threes also tend to blame their problems on other people, unable to recognize the part they have played in the situation.

WINGS

An Enneagram Three has a Two (the Helper) wing and a Four (the Individualist) wing. Most people have a stronger wing, but you do have access to both of your wings. Let's talk about some defining characteristics of the Three's wings.

A Three with a stronger Two wing is generally more helpful and giving of their time, energy, and resources. They are more people-oriented, social, and adaptable to many situations. They like the attention they receive from others more than those who have a Four wing. A Three with a Two wing will also be more competitive than other Threes because of their focus on appearances.

A Three with a Four wing will be more creative, artistic, and unique. They focus more on standing out from the crowd because

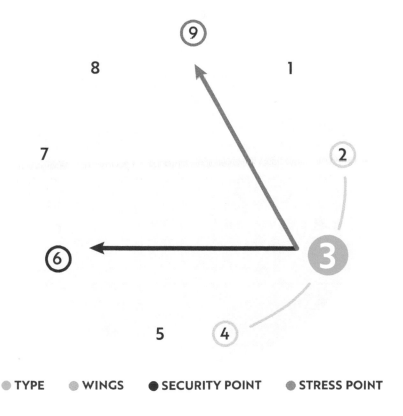

● TYPE ● WINGS ● SECURITY POINT ● STRESS POINT

of their unique abilities, rather than just their achievements. A Three with a Four wing is quieter and more focused on their emotions and feelings. They may be more sensitive to their feelings about their achievements specifically, and they may be focused on becoming the best at a specific skill set.

WHAT'S EASY FOR ACHIEVERS

Enneagram Threes excel at setting and achieving goals. It's easy for Achievers to finish projects and meet deadlines because they are driven by the motivation to succeed. They value results, no matter whether the project is big or small. Threes are really good at encouraging others. Because achievements are important to them, they want to see other people succeed as well. Indeed, they want to get to the top, but they want you right beside them. It's easy for Threes to see a project or situation and know what needs to be done to complete it. They are task-oriented and willing to get the job done, no matter what it takes.

WHAT'S HARD FOR ACHIEVERS

It's difficult for Achievers to separate work life from home life. Because they feel like they must constantly be striving for their definition of success, it's hard for them to release that mentality. This can look like an inability to shut their laptop at night or a struggle to set work-home boundaries. Threes also struggle with knowing who they are outside of their achievements. They may struggle with their identity because it has always been tied to the things they do. They are known to adjust who they are based on who others expect them to be. Failure is also very difficult for Achievers to accept. They may not even attempt to do things unless they know they will succeed.

HEALTHY BEHAVIORS

An Enneagram Three's desire to be valued leads to behaviors such as being extremely motivated and driven. When they value themselves, they are confident in who they are and what they have to offer. Because Threes want to be respected by others, they want to make sure that other people feel that same respect, so they will encourage them to go after what they want. Threes are optimistic and typically inspire others to achieve great things. They are charismatic and social, with an ability to hold conversations with anyone. They adapt to any situation they are in and view it as a personal challenge to do so. Threes work hard and know how to get the job done. When they are at their absolute best, they can be an important role model to others.

UNHEALTHY BEHAVIORS

When Enneagram Threes only focus on getting ahead, they can become fixated on doing it themselves instead of encouraging others to achieve alongside them. This can lead to extreme self-focus and vanity. Threes have a fear of failure that may cause them to believe that they are the only ones who can accomplish the task. Because of their desire for success, they can be overly competitive and do whatever they can to be sure to win. In trying to earn the respect of others, Threes tend to be workaholics because they have associated their identity with everything they can get done. Sometimes Threes can be so concerned about appearances that they don't want to show their authentic self.

WORK LIFE

Enneagram Threes are all about that work life. Even if a Three doesn't "work" in the traditional sense, they typically have some sort of job to do. You can trust a Three to always achieve what they have set out to accomplish, especially when it has to do with work. They set big goals and won't stop until they are met. It may seem like they are exceedingly competitive with others, and they can be at times. However, it's important to recognize that Threes are mostly competitive with themselves.

FAMILY LIFE

Enneagram Threes value relationships with their family members. They love to have fun, play games, and keep life exciting. They excel at encouraging their family members to be the best that they can be and to never give up. Like other areas of their lives, Threes sometimes feel a need to prove themselves to their family members. As a child, this can look like a desire to earn good grades. As an adult, this can look like wanting to excel at whatever job they have. This comes from a deep-rooted need to be valued by others. They have a hard time accepting that their family members love and value them regardless of their achievements. If you have a family member who is a Three, remind them to slow down and take breaks from working. Tell them that their value has nothing to do with what they achieve and that they are awesome just the way they are.

RELATIONSHIP LIFE

People are often drawn to Enneagram Threes because of their charming nature. This magnetic charm works the same way in their relationships. Threes want to be valued and respected by their partner, and they want their partner, friends, and family members to be proud of them. They may want to achieve things just for others' validation. In relationships, Threes can be who their partner needs them to be at any given moment. They adapt to situations and read what is required of them. Additionally, Threes are really good at encouraging their partners, friends, and family members to be the best version of themselves, and they will do whatever it takes to help them get there. They are generally caring, optimistic, and validating. If you are in a relationship with a Three, be a safe place for them to remove the "mask" and encourage them to show you their true self.

ACHIEVERS AND OTHER ENNEAGRAM TYPES

Achievers tend to get along well with other Enneagram types because of their ability to adapt to who other people need them to be. Here are some dynamics you might see in relationships with an Enneagram Three.

WITH ONES:
Threes and Ones both value getting things done and doing things well. However, there may be a struggle between them when defining the other's role.

WITH TWOS:
Threes and Twos are similar because Twos know what other people need, whereas Threes know who others need them to be. They are very supportive of each other and love to cheer each other on.

WITH THREES:
Threes really understand each other's desire to achieve, and they will always strive to be the best. However, they may struggle with competing with each other.

WITH FOURS:
Threes and Fours definitely have complementary strengths, but they also require a lot of validation from each other.

WITH FIVES:
Threes and Fives can seem similar at times because they both want to be competent and capable. They can both be emotionally disconnected at times, so communication between them can be difficult.

WITH SIXES:
Threes and Sixes are connected on the Enneagram, which makes mutual understanding a little easier for them. Both appreciate relationships and adhere to core values.

WITH SEVENS:
Sevens and Threes are good at encouraging those around them and always looking at the bright side of things. However, they both tend to avoid any sort of negative feelings.

WITH EIGHTS:
Power struggles between Threes and Eights may occur because they are both strong-willed and determined. However, they can understand that about each other.

WITH NINES:
Threes and Nines can also understand each other because they are connected on the Enneagram. They both seek out comfort; however, they need to watch out for their people-pleasing tendencies.

Achiever Mantras

When things get tough or whenever you feel like it, repeat these mantras and affirmations out loud or in your head to help center yourself. You can repeat one or say them one after another.

I am worth more than my achievements.

I can rest without feeling guilty.

I can be true to myself.

I can celebrate the accomplishments of others.

I am ready to learn from failure.

ACHIEVER EXERCISE

The goal of this exercise is to work toward discovering your true identity. Enneagram Threes often identify themselves through the role they take on. However, it's important to know who you are as an individual, not who you think others need or want you to be.

1. Create two columns. In one column, list the different roles you take on, such as parent, child, neighbor, etc. In the other column, list all the characteristics you have, such as helpful, giving, motivating, etc.

2. Match each characteristic to a role. You can match characteristics to as many roles as you see fit. Now look at all the characteristics that overlap between roles. Do they help you see who you are beyond the individual roles you take on? If you eliminated all those roles, who would you be?

3. Write down characteristics that you may have that don't necessarily align with any of the roles listed.

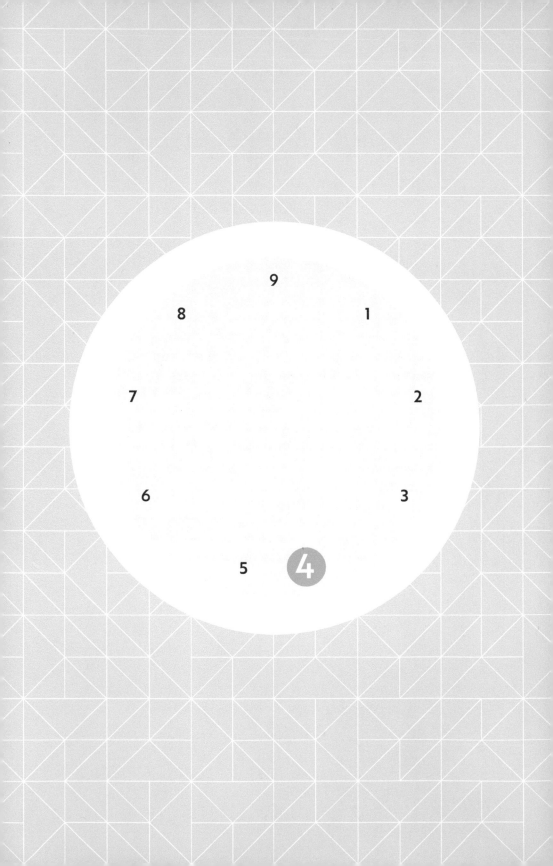

The Individualist

HOW INDIVIDUALISTS ACT

Enneagram Fours, or Individualists, are known for being focused on authenticity and being true to themselves. They tend to gravitate toward romanticism and creativity, which is why they are sometimes referred to as the Romantic or the Artist. Individualists seek a deep connection with everyone they meet. Wanting to understand others, they naturally find ways to learn about the deepest unknown parts of others' lives and personalities. They are in tune with their feelings and typically make decisions based on their emotions. Fours are on a quest to create meaning and significance in life. This can look like savoring small moments, like sunsets or a rainy day, or doing what they can to make a difference in the world.

MOTIVATIONS

Enneagram Fours are motivated by a desire to create an identity within themselves. This typically appears as wanting to be different from other people in a unique and significant way. Because of this, Fours typically want to engage in behaviors that are different from others. Fours are also motivated by a fear of being seen as defective. They want to be different, but not flawed. They strive to make sure that they are not the "black sheep" of the situation or relationship. They also fear not having personal significance or a purpose in life. For this reason, Fours often seek out opportunities to create meaning and find their purpose. They value deep connections because it feels like it is their purpose to connect with others in a meaningful way.

STRESS AND SECURITY POINTS

When healthy or in a state of security, Fours will engage in the positive traits of a One, the Reformer. However, when stressed or not in a healthy place, they will take on the negative qualities of a Two, the Helper.

When Fours are in a place of growth or security, they are more structured and organized like a One. They become more emotionally balanced and focused on doing the right thing. They tend to be more concerned with being a good person and focused on the role they can play in fighting for what is right.

When stressed, Fours start to feel like people aren't showing love to them in the way that they desire. This replicates the unhealthy behaviors of a Two, causing them to become possessive of their relationships and envious when they don't receive enough attention. Because Fours are trying to win the affection of others, they can become needy and overly accommodating to the people around them.

WINGS

The numbers on either side of an Enneagram Four are Three (the Achiever) and Five (the Investigator), making these a Four's wings. Most people will have a stronger wing, but part of growth work is to incorporate traits and qualities from both of the wings. There are significant differences between a Four with a strong Three wing and a Four with a strong Five wing.

A Four with a Three wing is also called the Aristocrat. Historically, an aristocrat is a member of an elite class. The Three wing brings out more of a focus on refined tastes or aesthetics because of the importance of appearances to that type. More focused on the things they can accomplish, they tend to work toward achieving goals. They are more extroverted than other Fours and oftentimes compare themselves to others who have what they

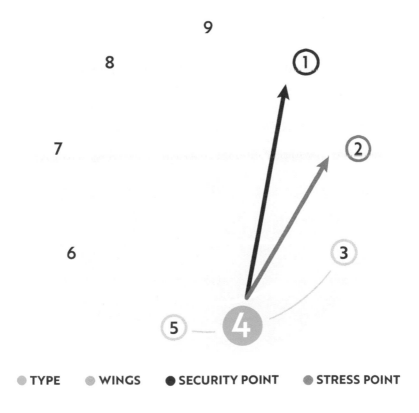

● TYPE　● WINGS　● SECURITY POINT　● STRESS POINT

want. A Four with a Three wing struggles with envy but is more focused on making a difference in the world.

A Four with a Five wing is referred to as the Bohemian. This type tends to be quieter and more withdrawn than the average Four. They also feel like they need to protect their emotions from other people, so they keep them to themselves. Even though they still make decisions based on how they feel about something, they need time to process those feelings. Fours with a Five wing are less dependent on others to meet their needs. They are more creative and rely on their intellectual side when deciding what to do.

WHAT'S EASY FOR INDIVIDUALISTS

Because of their desire to be understood, it comes naturally to Enneagram Fours to seek to understand others. Fours are empathetic, especially when it comes to others' feelings and emotions. Fours are also good at being authentically true to themselves and what they have to offer. They will never pretend to be someone that they are not; they want to be unique and significant. Fours also naturally know how to create deep and meaningful relationships with others, and they understand what others need to also be authentically themselves.

WHAT'S HARD FOR INDIVIDUALISTS

Enneagram Fours struggle with a sense of lacking or that something is missing; as a result, they also struggle with comparing themselves to other people. Because of this, Fours can have a hard time overcoming the shame they may experience. This shame is typically related to not feeling like they are "enough" for others. Fours also have a hard time receiving criticism. Even if people try to label it as constructive, a Four will have a hard time taking it in a positive way. They dislike being misunderstood and often retreat into their emotions when they feel like people don't take the time to truly get to know them.

HEALTHY BEHAVIORS

An Enneagram Four's tendency to try and understand others leads to empathy and sensitivity to others' emotional needs. Their ability to tune into their own emotional needs can lead them to rely on themselves for their own happiness instead of relying on others. Authenticity is extremely important to Fours. When they can truly be honest with themselves about how they are feeling and what they need, they can inspire others to do the same. True transformation into the best version of themselves can come from a Four's ability to be content with what they have. It can also come from being happy for what others have, even if it's something they themselves have not attained.

UNHEALTHY BEHAVIORS

Enneagram Fours can get stuck in a rut if they constantly fixate on what is missing in their lives. This often leads to envy and comparisons to other people. If Fours feel like they aren't being understood by others, they try to make others understand them. This can look like being needy or overly emotional to others. Fours often struggle with engaging in negative self-talk and being hard on themselves. This can lead them down a dark path if they are constantly withdrawing into their emotions. Some Fours may feel like they have to compensate for "not being enough," and in turn, they may isolate themselves from other people.

WORK LIFE

It's important for Enneagram Fours to establish a personal connection to the work they are doing. They won't begin a new job or career unless they are emotionally invested. Similar to other areas of their lives, Fours value transparency and authenticity. This is especially true of people who work in leadership positions. Fours want to make sure that other people are being as real as they are with them. Fours create deep and lasting connections with coworkers and colleagues. They can offer understanding in a unique way, and they are able to encourage others to speak their truth, even when it's uncomfortable. Fours struggle with receiving any sort of criticism. They are known to take things personally and can withdraw into their emotions. When this happens, they can appear moody, depressed, or self-absorbed. If interacting with a Four in the workplace, be transparent and seek to understand them as a whole.

FAMILY LIFE

Just like in other areas of their life, Enneagram Fours want to be understood by their family members. Family members have the ability to form intimate and deep connections, and Fours thrive in those relationships. Family members should understand that Fours appreciate a home environment with an aesthetic that allows them to feel comfortable. Fours will encourage their family members to be aware of their own feelings and emotions and not be afraid to share them. They will demonstrate significant empathy when a family member is going through a challenge. However, Fours often feel like they are the family member who doesn't quite fit in. Because they sometimes feel like something is wrong with them, it's easy for them to feel like an outcast at family events and get-togethers. They may feel as if their relatives don't understand them. Fours may also feel like their family members are judging them for their emotions. It's important for relatives to demonstrate that they accept them for who they are and how they feel.

RELATIONSHIP LIFE

Sometimes the Enneagram Four is also referred to as the Romantic because of their strong feelings. They also tend to idealize romance and all the feelings associated with it. Because of this, Fours tend to go all-in when seeking relationships with others. Fours bring an exceptional passion to all relationships, and they want their partners and friends to feel as much as they do. They will not enter into surface-level relationships at all, seeking only deep and meaningful connections. Sometimes the greatest joy for a Four is to be able to just sit and have conversations filled with depth and mutual understanding. However, when a Four becomes stressed in a relationship, they can become needy and overly emotional to make sure that other people need them. It is important that Fours recognize when they may be moving into those behaviors. If you're in a relationship with a Four, validate their passions and listen to their feelings and desires.

INDIVIDUALISTS AND OTHER ENNEAGRAM TYPES

Individualists get along well with others because of their passion and ability to deeply understand another's feelings and emotions. Here are some dynamics you might see in relationships with an Enneagram Four.

WITH ONES:
Fours and Ones typically share a desire to fulfill a higher purpose. They want to make a difference in the world. This similarity can help them understand one another.

WITH TWOS:
Twos and Fours get along well with each other, especially because they are connected on the Enneagram. They both demonstrate significant empathy and understanding of others.

WITH THREES:

Threes and Fours share a wing, enabling them to relate to each other more than other Enneagram types. They typically have strengths that complement each other, but they both need ample validation.

WITH FOURS:

Fours share an intensity and passion that only they can understand. They are sensitive to one another's needs and can understand each other's strong emotions.

WITH FIVES:

Fours and Fives both enjoy their independence and time apart from each other. However, Fours feel their own emotions strongly, whereas Fives may struggle to identify their own emotions.

WITH SIXES:

Fours and Sixes share a playfulness and warmth. However, they both tend to fear abandonment, which can get in the way if not addressed.

WITH SEVENS:

Both Fours and Sevens have a desire for adventure and imagination. The Four can help the Seven work through their emotions instead of running away from them.

WITH EIGHTS:

Fours and Eights value being true to themselves, and they will never try to be someone they aren't. They will both be passionate with each other; however, they will share it differently. They can both be strong-willed and may be stubborn when together.

WITH NINES:

Fours and Nines both demonstrate significant empathy toward others. They will seek to understand each other in a deep way; however, they can be stubborn and indecisive at times.

Individualist Mantras

When things get tough or whenever you feel like it, repeat these mantras and affirmations out loud or in your head to help center yourself. You can repeat one or say them one after another.

I appreciate the present moment.

I understand and love myself fully.

I can use my experiences to grow.

I bring beauty to others' lives.

My strong feelings do not control me.

INDIVIDUALIST EXERCISE

The goal of this exercise is to stop constantly comparing yourself to others. Part of this is to acknowledge what you do have, as well as to celebrate other people and what they have to offer. This will turn your mind away from thinking about what you don't have and make you feel more confident by turning your insecurity into validation.

1. To begin this exercise, write down everything that you *do* have. Consider materialistic things, relationships, and successes in your life.

2. After you spend time doing this, become aware of your feelings of comparison. When you find yourself comparing yourself to others, think about when these feelings arise, how they make you feel, and what the root of that feeling is.

3. Instead of withdrawing into your emotions, celebrate the person you are comparing yourself to in some way, shape, or form. Consider the effort they put into their success. Reflect on your own ability to recognize their gifts and the way you feel when somebody recognizes yours. Then validate them. Invite them to go out for coffee. Tell them you are happy for them. With practice, you'll really mean it and it will feel good!

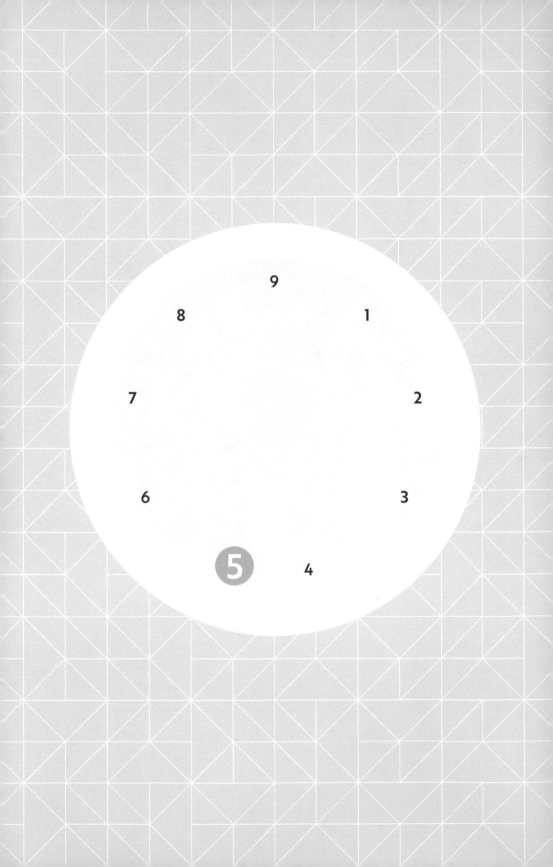

The Investigator

HOW INVESTIGATORS ACT

Enneagram Fives are also known as the Investigator or the Researcher. They are focused on gaining insight and knowledge about every topic they encounter. They don't just want to be knowledgeable; they want to be the one that people go to for information. Focused on independence, Fives value time spent alone, and they withdraw to process when things become overwhelming. Investigators seek to become experts in a specific area or master a body of knowledge. I like to refer to them as "walking search engines." They typically have a vast understanding of many different things, and they like it that way.

MOTIVATIONS

Investigators are motivated by a desire to be knowledgeable, but they also want to be perceived as competent and capable. They directly correlate having knowledge to being competent. This motivation leads Fives to ensure that they know everything there is to know about a topic. Investigators are also motivated by a fear of being seen as helpless, so they act like they don't need help from others. They also fear that their energy will be depleted from having so many obligations placed on them. Because of this, they try to have as few obligations placed on them as possible. They are more comfortable as an observer than an active participant.

STRESS AND SECURITY POINTS

When secure, Enneagram Fives demonstrate the positive qualities of an Eight, the Challenger. When stressed, Fives can show unhealthy qualities of a Seven, the Enthusiast. For those familiar with these types, it is obvious when a Five is stressed or in growth.

When Fives are in a healthy place, they become more decisive, confident, and capable of asserting themselves, all healthy traits of Eights. When this occurs, they can rely more on their gut instinct than having to process and think through everything. The healthy Eight is also revealed by a Five's ability to set and maintain their boundaries.

When stressed, Fives will demonstrate unhealthy qualities of a Seven, which includes getting easily distracted and overwhelmed. A Five will also become more impatient and annoyed with other people, especially when they are infringing on their boundaries. When stressed, Fives will act more impulsively and take on too many things at once.

WINGS

The numbers on either side of an Enneagram Five are Four (the Individualist) and Six (the Loyalist). Most people have a wing that is stronger than the other, but there is a tendency to demonstrate qualities of both types.

A Five with a Four wing is called the Iconoclast, also known as a Skeptic or a Questioner. As their name suggests, they are the Five that is going to doubt things until proven. This Enneagram type will be more sensitive and emotional than the average Five. They can detach from their intellectual side and be more in tune with their feelings. A Five with a Four wing is also more creative and eccentric.

A Five with a Six wing is called the Problem Solver because of their ability to assess a situation and come up with practical ways

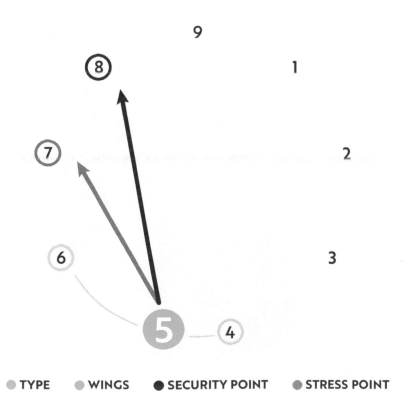

●TYPE　●WINGS　●SECURITY POINT　●STRESS POINT

to fix things. They do this by tapping into their intellectual side and observing the problem. This Enneagram type may be slightly more social than the traditional Five and seek security in others. A Five with a Six wing tends to research and analyze to get to the root of a problem.

WHAT'S EASY FOR INVESTIGATORS

Because of their need to gain as much information and knowledge as possible, Enneagram Fives excel at becoming experts on a specific topic. People know this about them and typically turn to them for wisdom and solutions. They possess good information and insight into many different areas. Fives also excel at setting and maintaining strong boundaries. They demonstrate exceptional skills at processing and thinking things through, and they often don't do anything without thinking it through fully.

WHAT'S HARD FOR INVESTIGATORS

Enneagram Fives struggle with social situations because it drains them. Because they fear depletion of their resources, they feel like they need to protect themselves from being drained. This leads them to put up strong walls and boundaries to keep people out. Because Fives want to gain as much knowledge as possible, they find it difficult if others know more than they do. Fives also have a harder time connecting with others on an emotional level. They are very cerebral and focused on intellect, so identifying their needs does not come naturally to them.

HEALTHY BEHAVIORS

Enneagram Fives' focus on gaining knowledge leads them to become competent and capable in specific areas of expertise. They are curious, perceptive, and inventive, as well as adept at seeking out ways to learn, grow, and develop. When they are confident in their ability to learn and grow, they are aware of their capacity to recharge so they will never be fully depleted. This allows them to confidently enter social situations without feeling overwhelmed.

UNHEALTHY BEHAVIORS

When Enneagram Fives are feeling overwhelmed for fear of becoming completely drained, they may withdraw and need to keep to themselves. This may cause them to put up extremely high walls to keep everyone out. Because of that need for privacy, some Fives fear that if they share even a little about themselves or what they are feeling, it will be too much. Because of their need to appear competent and knowledgeable, they try to make sure everyone sees that they know what they are talking about. This can come across to others as intellectual arrogance.

WORK LIFE

Enneagram Fives in the workplace are known for being analytical, and they are exceptionally good at strategizing and researching. Coworkers and colleagues know to seek this person out if they need an answer to something. Similar to other areas of their life, Fives value autonomy in the workplace. They tend to choose a job or career that allows them to work at their own pace, rely on themselves, and have the ability to recharge when that is just not possible. Fives typically love to keep their doors shut; they work better when they can simply focus on the task at hand. They tend to hide behind their knowledge because that feels safe to them, so it's important to remind them that they are more than just what they know. Fives can also struggle with opening up to people, which is understandable in a professional setting. However, that can lead to feelings of disconnectedness from coworkers and colleagues. If you interact with a Five in the workplace, make it known that you value them for more than just their knowledge and that they are competent even without having to obtain every single piece of information.

FAMILY LIFE

An Enneagram Five is the family member who typically is happy to sit in the background and observe what is going on around them. They tend to be more reserved and would rather listen to the conversations instead of fully engage. However, they are the family member who always has an answer to something you're curious about, and they love to share their knowledge with others. Because of their love of knowledge, they want to learn about their family members as well. Fives may feel more comfortable opening up to family members than when they are in other relationships; however, they may still have boundaries, as they are just private people in general. Fives are easily depleted by large social gatherings, and family events are no exception. If you have a family member who is a Five, allow them to have their space and work to respect their boundaries.

RELATIONSHIP LIFE

Relationships with Enneagram Fives are full of curiosity, mainly because Fives keep so much to themselves. However, they are loyal and understanding in their relationships with friends and partners. Fives appreciate independence in all areas of their lives, and it's the same with relationships. They appreciate partners and friends who allow them to spend time focusing on their own interests, and they want others to experience that freedom as well. This allows Fives to recharge before spending time with their partner again. It may seem that Fives don't have many needs, but they may just need to be uncovered. Fives struggle with communication at times, and they especially do not want to be seen as a burden. Working on communication barriers is helpful for breaking down walls. If you're in a relationship or friendship with a Five, know that they want to be there. They don't enter things that they aren't 100-percent sure about before they process everything. Just respect their boundaries.

INVESTIGATORS AND OTHER ENNEAGRAM TYPES

Enneagram Fives get along well with other Enneagram types because of their ability to offer independence and autonomy to their partners and friends. Here are some dynamics you might see in relationships with an Enneagram Five.

WITH ONES:
Fives and Ones get along well because they are both structured and logical thinkers. However, they can both be judgmental at times.

WITH TWOS:
Fives and Twos can balance each other out emotionally, but they have many differences. Twos want to feel needed, and Fives want to make sure they don't have needs.

WITH THREES:
Fives and Threes share a similar work ethic and desire to get things done. They are both self-reliant; however, Threes need a bit more validation than Fives do.

WITH FOURS:
Fours and Fives understand each other well because they are next to each other on the Enneagram. They are both open-minded and curious; however, Fours can be very sensitive to criticism.

WITH FIVES:
Fives understand another Five's need for privacy and independence. However, they might be inclined to compete to see who knows more.

WITH SIXES:
Fives and Sixes have a mutual desire for intellectual connection, and they will seek to understand each other. However, Sixes need to feel safe with others, and Fives may not be able to provide that level of comfort.

WITH SEVENS:
Fives and Sevens balance each other out at times, and they are connected on the Enneagram. They both value independence and doing things separately as well as together. However, Sevens can be much more energetic, which can leave Fives drained.

WITH EIGHTS:
Fives and Eights are also connected on the Enneagram, which leads to a unique mutual understanding. Both types are decisive and value independence. However, they can also be stubborn.

WITH NINES:
Fives and Nines respect each other's need for personal space and privacy. Nines have an understanding of Fives that others may not. However, both types avoid conflict.

Investigator Mantras

When things get tough or whenever you feel like it, repeat these mantras and affirmations out loud or in your head to help center yourself. You can repeat one or say them one after another.

I need others and others need me.

I stay engaged in my surroundings.

I know enough to move forward.

I choose compassion and seek understanding.

I choose to connect with others.

INVESTIGATOR EXERCISE

The purpose of this exercise is to help you understand how to connect with and identify your feelings and emotions. This can be hard for a Five to do, but those feelings and emotions are in there.

1. Choose several times of the day to take just one or two minutes to reflect. For example, maybe it's 9 a.m., 12 p.m., 3 p.m., and 6 p.m. Set an alarm on your phone to remind yourself to pause during those times.

2. At those times, pause and think:

   What am I feeling right now?

   Why am I feeling this way?

   How can I express how I'm feeling?

   Who do I trust to share these feelings and emotions with?

3. Do this for at least a week to practice identifying your feelings.

The Loyalist

HOW LOYALISTS ACT

Enneagram Sixes are also called Loyalists, and like their name suggests, they are devoutly loyal and committed to people, relationships, work environments, and everything else in their lives. Focused on safety, loyalists don't engage in many behaviors that are out of their comfort zone. Loyalists feel a sense of responsibility to those around them, which may look like being in a committed relationship or being community-oriented. Trust is important to them, but it does not come easily and it often takes time for them to open up. Sixes anticipate outcomes, which leads them to be prepared for anything.

MOTIVATIONS

Loyalists are motivated by a desire to seek guidance, safety, and security from those around them and from their environment. Their behaviors are directly connected to their need to be secure in whatever situation they are in. They may look to others for guidance when they are making big decisions or transitions. This also leads to Loyalists' connection with authority figures. Typically, they look to them for that guidance and security, or they go against them completely. Sixes are also motivated by a fear of fear itself. Fear is directly connected to not feeling safe and therefore acts as a motivator for doing the things they do. Sixes also fear losing guidance that they are receiving from someone or not feeling secure in their relationships or environment.

STRESS AND SECURITY POINTS

When healthy or in a place of growth, Enneagram Sixes will demonstrate the positive qualities of a Nine, the Peacemaker. When stressed, they will exhibit negative qualities of a Three, the Achiever.

When healthy, Sixes turn their fear into courage. They take on the healthy qualities of a Nine, as they become more empathetic and understanding of others. They are also more able to go with the flow and deal with things as they come instead of having to plan for all worst-case scenarios. They begin to trust themselves and their decisions more.

When stressed, Sixes take on the negative qualities of a Three, including becoming more self-focused and competitive and doing whatever it takes to get ahead. When stressed, Sixes spend a lot of effort focused on avoiding failure. They may reject new ideas or experiences because they are afraid to fail. Sixes, when stressed, may also think they are the only ones who can do something a certain way, which can come across as arrogance.

WINGS

The Enneagram types next to an Enneagram Six are Five (the Investigator) and Seven (the Enthusiast). These wings can each affect a Six in unique ways.

A Six with a Five wing is called the Defender because of their ability to use logic to defend the people they are closest to. At times, this type can look like a One or Eight because of their ability to fight for what they believe in and their ability to be organized and self-controlled. A Six with a Five wing will also be more outspoken than the traditional Six. They have strong values and beliefs and want to make sure they are known. However, a Six with a Five wing will also tend to isolate themselves more, especially when anxious or worried.

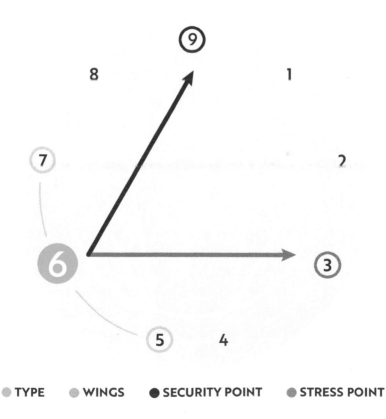

● TYPE   ● WINGS   ● SECURITY POINT   ● STRESS POINT

A Six with a Seven wing is called the Buddy. This type focuses more on their relationships and how they can be a supportive and likeable person. A Six with a Seven wing is more outgoing and sociable than the traditional Six, and they may engage in a wider variety of activities and experiences. They want to be known as a friend and the person who is always prepared for anything that comes their way. They are steady, loyal, and focused on working together for the greater good of everyone.

WHAT'S EASY FOR LOYALISTS

An Enneagram Six's greatest need is to feel safe and secure. Consequently, they are naturally skilled at anticipating what they need to do to maintain those feelings. This often looks like planning for multiple scenarios "just in case" and being prepared for anything that could happen. Sixes are also good at staying committed to things that are important to them. This could be personal relationships or work environments, but it could also be values, beliefs, and the things that they are passionate about. Like their name suggests, Sixes excel at being loyal in all settings.

WHAT'S HARD FOR LOYALISTS

Enneagram Sixes struggle with fear, worry, and anxiety because of their need to feel safe and secure. It's difficult for them to step outside their comfort zone because that is not the safe thing to do. It can also be exhausting for them to have to constantly anticipate what could go wrong and plan for worst-case scenarios. Sixes have a hard time trusting others, including and especially themselves. They sometimes become indecisive and wind up freezing, not able to make a decision at all. Sixes want to exert their confidence, but it's hard to do so with so many "what-ifs" circling in their mind.

HEALTHY BEHAVIORS

Enneagram Sixes' focus on safety and security often leads them to remain in comfortable situations. However, it also allows them to plan and prepare for things that could possibly make them feel uncomfortable. When Sixes step outside their comfort zone, they demonstrate a type of courage that no other Enneagram type has, simply because of their ability to overcome fear. Sixes can be confident in themselves and their decisions and be direct with other people. When they trust their own guidance, they can direct themselves on the path they want to take, instead of relying on others to guide them.

UNHEALTHY BEHAVIORS

When Enneagram Sixes are not able to trust themselves and their decisions, they rely on others by seeking guidance from them. They can become resentful when they feel like they aren't receiving that guidance. When they let others dictate the direction they're going in, they can become fearful of what's to come instead of gaining control of the situation and taking matters into their own hands. A lack of control can lead to some of the worry and anxiety that Sixes experience. This causes them to think about worst-case scenarios because they don't trust that their original scenario will work out. When this happens, they need to focus on building that confidence and trust in themselves, which can lead to true transformation.

WORK LIFE

Unsurprisingly, Enneagram Sixes in the workplace are known for being loyal. Sixes will often have longevity at a company, and it may be difficult for them to leave. Because they value safety and security, their work environment is no different. Safety and security can mean different things to people, but for a Six, it is related to comfort. Specifically, this is how comfortable they feel with the job that they have, the people who work there, and the company itself. Sixes excel at being prepared and creating solutions. They assist coworkers and colleagues in identifying the problem and figuring out how to fix it. Like in other areas, Sixes may struggle with self-doubt in the workplace. They have a difficult time trusting their decisions and their ability to succeed. If you are interacting with a Six in the workplace, remind them what an asset they are to the group and that they are capable of creating solutions.

FAMILY LIFE

Enneagram Sixes value relationships with their family members because of the established loyalty. Family relationships are important to Sixes because they feel comfortable to them. They've known them the longest and have an authenticated relationship. Family members appreciate the Six's ability to prepare for everything, from packing extra snacks to always remembering the sunscreen. They know that they can always count on a Six. Similar to other areas of their lives, Sixes may experience worry or anxiety, and a lot of the time it is related to the well-being of their family members. They typically keep this worry to themselves, and people don't even know they are experiencing it. Sixes are fiercely protective of their family and want to make sure they are safe and secure at all times. If you have a family member who is a Six, be sure to show them the same type of loyalty that they demonstrate toward you.

RELATIONSHIP LIFE

Similar to other areas of their lives, Sixes are extremely loyal as a friend or partner. They bring their own values and beliefs to the relationship, and they don't expect their partners or friends to change who they are. Sixes allow for the individuality that naturally occurs in relationships. Even though Sixes stereotypically tend to struggle with worry and anxiety, they are inherently playful and enjoy being silly. Enneagram Sixes are honest and reliable, and they follow through on their promises. They work to make sure they are meeting your needs and that you are taken care of at all times. Because of their propensity to struggle with worry and self-doubt, it is important that they receive that same love and care in return. If you are in any type of relationship with a Six, validate those worries and fears and help them overcome them.

LOYALISTS AND OTHER ENNEAGRAM TYPES

Enneagram Sixes get along well with other Enneagram types because of their immense loyalty and compassion for others. Here are some dynamics you might see in relationships with an Enneagram Six.

WITH ONES:
Sixes and Ones are both responsible and strive to do the right thing. They also both demonstrate loyalty. However, they can both be critical and sensitive to criticism.

WITH TWOS:
Sixes and Twos get along well because they both value relationships and are committed to each other. They can both struggle with procrastination at times.

WITH THREES:
Sixes and Threes can understand each other well because they are connected on the Enneagram. They are both service-oriented and like to see results. However, Sixes tend to be more indecisive.

WITH FOURS:
Sixes and Fours can be very supportive of each other and fulfill the other's needs. Sixes feel understood by Fours, and Fours feel taken care of by Sixes. However, when stressed, they can both be moody.

WITH FIVES:
Sixes and Fives can relate to each other well because they are next to each other on the Enneagram. They both desire to have their boundaries respected. Sixes appreciate the decisive nature of a Five because that doesn't come naturally to them.

WITH SIXES:
Sixes have a shared understanding of each other's worries and fears. They feel like the other person truly gets them. However, they can feed off of each other's anxieties and fears and get stuck, not knowing how to move forward.

WITH SEVENS:
Sixes and Sevens balance each other out in many ways. Sevens can pull Sixes out of their comfort zone, and Sixes can remind Sevens to slow down. However, a Seven could feel overwhelmed by a Six's fears and worries.

WITH EIGHTS:
Both Sixes and Eights are very protective of the people in their life. They share a passion for loyalty and honesty. However, they both struggle with trust at first, and it may take some time for them to open up to one another.

WITH NINES:
Sixes and Nines are connected on the Enneagram, and therefore they can understand one another's motivations. Comfort and peaceful environments are important to Sixes and Nines. However, they can both struggle with indecisiveness at times.

Loyalist Mantras

When things get tough or whenever you feel like it, repeat these mantras and affirmations out loud or in your head to help center yourself. You can repeat one or say them one after another.

I trust myself and my decisions.

I am safe in this moment.

I am grounded in my being.

I am in control of my life.

I am well supported and loved by others.

LOYALIST EXERCISE

The purpose of this exercise is to learn how to trust your mind, body, and gut instinct. You have the knowledge to be able to do this; you just need to put it into action. By trusting yourself, you can step into a newfound confidence.

1. Think about all the times you have been able to trust yourself. Consider things that have gone well for you: decisions you've made, steps you've taken. Remember, you have done this before. Write them down if you wish.

2. Next, think about things that have gone wrong, specifically after relying on someone else. When you think of an event, ask yourself:

   Did you seek counsel from someone and it didn't go well?

   Did you trust someone to complete their part?

   Why do you trust others more than you trust yourself?

   What are you missing by not stepping out into courage or trusting yourself?

The Enthusiast

HOW ENTHUSIASTS ACT

Enneagram Sevens, or Enthusiasts, are typically the most out-going on the Enneagram. Like their name suggests, they are enthusiastic and energetic, and they maintain a positive out-look on life. Enthusiasts love to engage in new experiences and adventures because they don't like being bored. They excel at generating new ideas because of their creativity and ability to think outside the box. Sevens often avoid any sort of negativity, which can lead to them burying difficult or painful experiences. They encourage people to look at the glass as half-full, and they radiate sunshine wherever they go.

MOTIVATIONS

Enneagram Sevens are motivated by a desire to have fun and experience new things, but they also seek contentment. They are quick to move on or generate new ideas or adventures because they want to be content. It's difficult for Sevens to be content in the moment that they are in. Enthusiasts are also motivated by a fear of missing out. However, they are mostly afraid of being trapped in emotional pain because they avoid negativity. They tend to avoid any emotional pain and hardship by doing the things that bring them the most joy and happiness. This can lead to them never actually dealing with the hard things, thus continuing to struggle for years to come.

STRESS AND SECURITY POINTS

When in an unhealthy place or a state of stress, Enneagram Sevens tend to take on the negative qualities of a One, the Reformer. However, they can also access the positive qualities of a Five, the Investigator, which is where they go when they are in a place of growth.

When stressed, Sevens exhibit negative qualities of a One, becoming critical and judgmental of others and feeling a need to strive for perfection. They get overly focused on others' imperfections, and they become more structured, placing limitations on themselves and what they can do.

When in a healthy place or a place of growth, Sevens have access to the positive qualities of a Five. This enables them to slow down, rest, and focus their attention on gaining knowledge and wisdom. They are also able to access all qualities of life. In this case, it means they don't run away from negativity; rather, they accept it for what it is.

WINGS

An Enneagram Seven has a Six (the Loyalist) wing and an Eight (the Challenger) wing. Both of these types make the traditional Enneagram Seven look a little different, depending on which wing is stronger.

A Seven with a Six wing is more subdued than an average Seven. More focused on relationships, they have a strong desire to experience new things with others. They are very committed to their people and expect others to be that way in return. A Seven with a Six wing still craves adventure, but they may think it through a bit more than a traditional Seven.

A Seven with an Eight wing is more decisive and direct. They are less concerned with what people think about them because they don't want to waste time with the opinions of others.

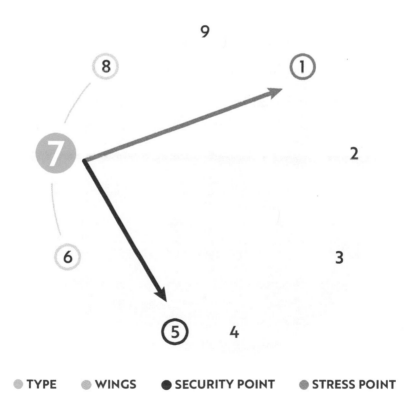

● TYPE　　● WINGS　　● SECURITY POINT　　● STRESS POINT

A Seven with an Eight wing is more confident, and they may even appear intense in their energy level.

WHAT'S EASY FOR ENTHUSIASTS

Enthusiasts are naturals at finding the bright side in every situation. They are always able to find something positive when negativity starts to creep in. It's also natural for Sevens to encourage their people and cheer them on in life. Like their name suggests, they are enthusiastic when it comes to helping others see all that life has to offer. It's easy for them to view the glass as half-full because negativity is just not an option for them. Being social comes easily to Sevens because of their love of people and adventures.

WHAT'S HARD FOR ENTHUSIASTS

Any sort of negativity is extremely hard for Enthusiasts. They avoid anything that is going to bring them down and bury it for as long as humanly possible. They also struggle with feeling like there is not enough time in the day to do all the things they want to do. This can lead to overbooking their schedule and being unable to slow down. Sevens may also struggle with follow-through. They are great at generating new ideas, but the completion of that idea may be difficult. This is because a Seven's mind is constantly thinking about the next thing.

HEALTHY BEHAVIORS

An Enneagram Seven's ability to view the positive side of things leads them to inspire others. Their positive energy can almost be contagious, as others can't help but also view things in a positive light when they look at things from the Seven's perspective. However, when Sevens accept negativity for what it is, they are able to be the healthiest version of themselves; here they are able to let go of the expectations that they have of themselves to always be happy and on the go all the time. A Seven's need to experience new things makes them confident, full of adventure, and seemingly able to take on the world. Because they are naturally curious, they seek to find answers and understand what life has to offer.

UNHEALTHY BEHAVIORS

When Enneagram Sevens are not content, they are constantly doing things to find fulfillment. They will quickly move on from whatever situation and experience they are in. Unable to slow down, they are only focused on themselves and what they can do to avoid any sort of negativity. Because of their need to be on the go, they are prone to burnout and becoming run-down. Sevens may not be able to be present, but instead may prefer to live in a fantasy world deep in their imagination. As a result, Sevens may find themselves feeling like they will never be able to find contentment or figure out what they want out of life.

WORK LIFE

It's easy to spot an Enneagram Seven in the workplace because of the energy and creativity that surrounds them. Like in other areas of their lives, Sevens are extremely positive in the workplace. They are able to spin failures or mistakes into a learning experience and to see the positive that comes from them. In the workplace specifically, they excel at generating new ideas and multiple solutions. They are quick thinkers and can act on new ideas impulsively. Sevens typically stand out as that colleague who wants to celebrate everything. They love to find out information about their coworkers and generate conversations. They also want to know how to best encourage their coworkers and colleagues. Sevens in the workplace may struggle with staying focused because their mind tends to move in various directions.

If you work with a Seven, it's important to help them redirect their focus back to whatever they are working on at that moment.

FAMILY LIFE

If you have a family member who is an Enneagram Seven, they are likely the ones who are constantly telling jokes and making other people laugh. They encourage their family members to be positive and look on the bright side, even in the darkest of times. They inspire their families to live life to the fullest and dream big dreams. Sevens will ensure that the family does not lack adventure and exciting times. This could look like planning extravagant vacations or making sure their weekends are booked with fun things to do. Because Sevens often have a difficult time focusing, they may find it hard to stay present in a serious conversation with family members, especially if there is any sort of negativity involved. Because Sevens avoid negativity altogether, they may bury how they are feeling about things and focus only on positive emotions. One thing is for sure, though: There is never a dull moment if you have a family member who is a Seven.

RELATIONSHIP LIFE

When Sevens are in a romantic relationship, they are extremely committed. However, it can be difficult for Sevens to get there because of their fear of being tied down. They need to have freedom and independence in a romantic relationship in order for it to work. Sevens bring a lot of fun and excitement to romantic relationships. They are caring and generous, and they love to encourage their partners to chase after their dreams. They are their partner's biggest cheerleader, and they want to feel that in return. Sevens may have a difficult time slowing down and need to be reminded that there is more to life than constantly being on the go.

If you are in a relationship with a Seven, remind them that there is a lot to be seen in the simple things in life as well.

Remind them that they can slow down and take it all in, and that they aren't missing out on anything if they decide to do that. If you're in a relationship with a Seven, you can guarantee that there is always fun to be had.

ENTHUSIASTS AND OTHER ENNEAGRAM TYPES

Enneagram Sevens are generally easy to get along with, thanks to their positive outlook. Here are some dynamics you might see in relationships with an Enneagram Seven.

WITH ONES:
Sevens and Ones can be very supportive of each other because they balance each other out. Ones can help Sevens to be more principled, and Sevens can help Ones to live life to the fullest.

WITH TWOS:
Sevens and Twos can look similar at times. However, Twos can help Sevens learn to express their feelings, whereas Sevens can help Twos learn how to do what they really want to do.

WITH THREES:
Threes and Sevens both have a lot of energy and excel at generating ideas. However, Threes can encourage Sevens to be more focused on the end goal.

WITH FOURS:
Fours and Sevens look alike at times because they are both creative and eclectic. However, Sevens want to avoid all negativity, whereas Fours like to experience sadness at times.

WITH FIVES:
Fives and Sevens can understand each other because they are connected on the Enneagram. Fives can remind Sevens to slow down and rest, and Sevens can pull Fives out of their comfort zone.

WITH SIXES:
Sevens and Sixes balance each other out because they both spend a lot of time in their heads. Sevens excel at generating ideas, and Sixes help put ideas into motion.

WITH SEVENS:
Sevens generate an immense amount of energy and positivity together. They may struggle with addressing conflict or negativity.

WITH EIGHTS:
Sevens and Eights can understand each other well because they are next to each other on the Enneagram. They are both passionate and independent. Sevens can remind Eights to let loose and have fun.

WITH NINES:
Sevens and Nines can relate because they both avoid conflict and negativity. Sevens can help Nines step out of their comfort zone, and Nines can help Sevens relax and slow down.

Enthusiast Mantras

When things get tough or whenever you feel like it, repeat these mantras and affirmations out loud or in your head to help center yourself. You can repeat one or say them one after another.

I am right where I'm supposed to be.

I trust myself.

I am content with what I have.

I am free to be me.

I am grateful for everything.

ENTHUSIAST EXERCISE

The goal of this exercise is to address any negativity or hard emotions that you may have been avoiding. As we know, Sevens tend to focus on all the positive things in life and bury any sort of emotional pain that they are experiencing. By continuing to do this, Sevens aren't able to work through the difficult things. It's okay to feel like this is out of your comfort zone, but it's helpful to embrace those emotions. Because you've been ignoring it for so long, this may be difficult to do at first.

1. Instead of focusing just on the positive things that have happened, reflect on things that you didn't love about your day. Identify one negative thing that you may be experiencing.

2. You may do something else while you're thinking about these emotions, such as listening to music, going for a walk, or being in a safe and comfortable place. Whatever you do, don't criticize yourself for feeling uncomfortable.

3. Do this for a week and get comfortable with feeling uncomfortable at times. The more you face uncomfortable feelings or issues, the more likely you are to work through them and find solutions.

The Challenger

HOW CHALLENGERS ACT

Enneagram Eights, or Challengers, are outspoken and assertive and like to be in charge. They demonstrate exceptional leadership qualities because of their ability to delegate and get things done. Challengers are extremely independent and don't want to rely on others to meet their needs. Focused on protecting themselves and others, they strive to make sure that people aren't being taken advantage of by standing up for the underdog. Eights are quick to make decisions, and they rely on their gut instinct to confirm that they are doing the right thing. Eights often have a strong exterior that masks a vulnerable interior that they don't want people to see.

MOTIVATIONS

Enneagram Eights are motivated by a desire to protect themselves and others. This often comes across as a need to be in control. If they maintain control, they can protect themselves. Eights also have a desire to maintain their independence in order to feel strong and capable. This is because they fear being seen as weak, powerless, or controlled in some way. Eights may believe that showing emotions or feelings is a sign of weakness. They tend to resist vulnerability because they don't want to be seen that way by others. They also want to protect others by making sure they feel equipped to stand up for themselves.

STRESS AND SECURITY POINTS

Typically, Enneagram Eights exhibit the negative qualities of a Five, the Investigator, when stressed or in an unhealthy spot. However, Eights can access the positive qualities of a Two, the Helper, when in growth.

When stressed, Eights will take on the negative qualities of a Five, the Investigator, by withdrawing and isolating themselves from others. They put up high walls and strong boundaries to protect themselves. When stressed, they can also start to lose trust in others and rely only on themselves.

When healthy or in a good place, Eights can exhibit the positive qualities of a Two by using their strength to help improve the lives of others. They will also put others' needs before their own and be very altruistic. At these times, they are more in tune with their emotions and more empathetic of others.

WINGS

An Enneagram Eight has a Seven (the Enthusiast) wing and a Nine (the Peacemaker) wing. These wings have a tendency to be very different from one another and can drastically change the characteristics of the Eight itself. However, it's important to remember that the primary motivation will always remain in the main Enneagram type.

An Eight with a strong Seven wing is more outgoing and energetic than the stereotypical Eight. They are typically more blunt and direct. Eights with a Seven wing are extremely quick thinkers and can be more impulsive and quick to make decisions.

An Eight with a Nine wing may be quieter than the traditional Eight. They are often able to deal with conflict, but they don't necessarily want to. Eights with a Nine wing are more patient and compassionate than those with a Seven wing. They are more focused on comfort and have a gentle strength.

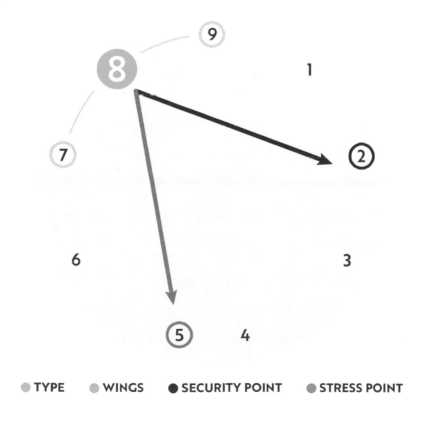

● TYPE   ● WINGS   ● SECURITY POINT   ● STRESS POINT

WHAT'S EASY FOR CHALLENGERS

Challengers are direct with their words and behaviors. You never have to wonder where you stand with them or how they are feeling about something. Eights also excel in leadership positions. Their willingness to do the tough jobs and stand up for the vulnerable is inspiring to others. Because of their strong personality and decisive nature, people naturally look up to them. Eights are also good at handling conflict if it comes their way. They don't back down from a fight, and they expect others to have that same mentality.

WHAT'S HARD FOR CHALLENGERS

Enneagram Eights really struggle with relinquishing control. For most Eights, control isn't about controlling other people. Control is about knowing the plan, sticking to the plan, and having things go their way. Eights struggle with being flexible and making adjustments when things don't go as planned. Eights also have trouble with people who don't know how to effectively use their voice. They wish that other people could be as direct as they are, and they don't understand why people don't just say what they mean. It's hard for Eights to realize that people aren't always going to do things the way that they do.

HEALTHY BEHAVIORS

An Eight's protective nature can lead them to exhibit qualities that leave an impact on others. Their need to improve the world around them makes them a driving force for change. Eights want everyone to have a voice. They encourage others to speak their truth and stand strong on their own. Eights are natural leaders in all of their environments, and they show compassion and gentle strength to those around them. Because of their desire to serve others in an impactful way, they are gentle and caring to those who need it most.

UNHEALTHY BEHAVIORS

When Enneagram Eights are unable to protect themselves and others, they do whatever they can to regain that protection. This can often look like a need to be in control of their environment. Eights have a tendency to put up high walls to keep people out, especially if they have already had their boundaries crossed. Because Eights are so focused on not appearing weak, they can sometimes come across as overly competitive or aggressive. To Eights, weakness is associated with powerlessness, so they will make sure they remain in control and in a powerful position.

WORK LIFE

Enneagram Eights are the natural leaders that colleagues and coworkers look up to and seek out for guidance. It's easy to tell if an Eight is in the room because they radiate a powerful presence and make it known that they like to be in charge. People will never have to wonder where they stand with an Eight because Eights have no problem speaking their mind; they are brutally honest, especially if they are seeking change in a specific area. Eights shine at getting things done. Supervisors, coworkers, and colleagues know to go to them if they need someone to help them view the big picture. Eights also know how to delegate if needed. They tend to struggle in the workplace when things don't go their way or they feel like things are out of their control. Eights need to learn how to adapt and move on when those situations occur. If you have a coworker or colleague who is an Eight, be direct with them and do what you say you are going to do.

FAMILY LIFE

Enneagram Eights are passionate about standing up for and protecting their family members. They also encourage their family members to stand up for themselves and what they believe in. Eights radiate a strong presence, even in the family structure. They are the leader of the family and like to be in charge of planning family activities or delegating tasks. Eights do not shy away from family debates or tense conversations; in fact, they look at them as a necessary component of a strong relationship. They sometimes possess a "my way or the highway" mentality and can be inflexible to change. However, their sharp tone of voice is typically due to passion, not anger. If you have a family member who is an Eight, try to be as honest and direct with them as they are with you. They respect that.

RELATIONSHIP LIFE

Enneagram Eights are full of passion in romantic relationships. They aren't just passionate about their partner, but about the relationship itself. They don't want to fail. Eights have no problem expressing their wants and desires, and oftentimes they wish that their partner would be as direct and honest in return. Similar to other Enneagram types, Eights need to have some independence and freedom in their relationships. Independence for them looks like being able to do activities and hobbies by themselves in addition to the things they do with their partner. Eights want the best for their partner, and they will empower them to achieve their goals and be who they want to be. However, Eights can often struggle with the need to maintain control, and they associate having needs with appearing weak. If you're in a relationship with an Eight, give them the independence they need, but also be a safe place for them to land and encourage them to let their walls down.

CHALLENGERS AND OTHER ENNEAGRAM TYPES

Enneagram Eights have a strong desire to protect the people around them, and this is often demonstrated in relationships. Here are some dynamics you might see in relationships with an Enneagram Eight.

WITH ONES:

Ones and Eights can be a powerful combination because of their focus on truth, honesty, and fighting against injustice. However, they can both be stubborn at times.

WITH TWOS:

Twos and Eights can balance each other out because they are connected on the Enneagram. Twos can help Eights be more in tune with their feelings and emotions, and Eights can help Twos learn how to stick up for themselves.

WITH THREES:

Threes and Eights can look very similar because of their shared determination and ability to get things done. Eights can help Threes learn to care less about what others think of them.

WITH FOURS:

Both Eights and Fours can be extremely passionate and intense. Fours can show Eights how to be more self-aware, and Eights can show Fours how to rely on their gut instinct.

WITH FIVES:

Fives and Eights typically have what the other needs. For example, Fives need someone to teach them how to be more direct and engaged in the world, whereas Eights need to learn how to slow down and think before reacting. This pairing really balances each other out.

WITH SIXES:
Sixes can often be a trusted advisor to an Eight by helping them think through multiple scenarios. Eights can help Sixes become more decisive.

WITH SEVENS:
Sevens and Eights enjoy experiencing new things. They are both independent and like to do things their own way, but they can push the other one away because of that.

WITH EIGHTS:
Two Eights may be an intense combination because of their shared relationship to control. They may experience conflict because of that. However, deep mutual appreciation exists for their shared traits of confidence, honesty, and protection.

WITH NINES:
Nines and Eights are opposite in a lot of ways, which can be a good thing. Eights can help Nines step into confidence and assert themselves. Nines offer a calm and stable environment for Eights.

Challenger Mantras

When things get tough or whenever you feel like it, repeat these mantras and affirmations out loud or in your head to help center yourself. You can repeat one or say them one after another.

Vulnerability is not weakness.

I can accept others' perspectives.

I trust myself and others.

I am strong and capable.

I am in control of my life.

CHALLENGER EXERCISE

The purpose of this exercise is to encourage Eights to pause and think about things before reacting. Eights rely on their gut instinct to make decisions, so they can be quite impulsive. This isn't always a negative thing; however, it can cause them to become impatient and demanding of others. It will be beneficial for Eights to train their brain to pause when they feel an impulse coming on by asking themselves why they want to react in that way.

1. Every time an impulse comes on, pause and ask yourself:

   Why do I need to take action right now?

   What is the worst that could happen if I don't take action immediately?

2. As you pause to reflect, you've interrupted your impulses to move forward. Now decide if it's worth it to take action, share that opinion, or speak those words.

3. Be gentle with yourself, as this may take some time. It doesn't have to work perfectly. Over time, you'll become more adept at this skill.

9

8

7

6

5   4

3

2

1

The Peacemaker

HOW PEACEMAKERS ACT

Enneagram Nines, or Peacemakers, are gentle, empathetic, and focused on maintaining peaceful environments. Peacemakers are typically able to go with the flow due to a desire to make sure everyone is okay and content. Nines are easy to approach and typically nonjudgmental toward the people they interact with. Peacemakers hate conflict and will avoid it at all costs because it disrupts the peaceful environment they are trying to maintain. Nines may have a hard time expressing their opinion or feelings if there is a chance that it could create conflict.

MOTIVATIONS

Enneagram Nines are motivated by a need to maintain their peaceful environment. Everything they do is designed to ensure that they are keeping the peace. As a rule, they want everyone to get along and for everyone to be happy and content. For this reason, they may have a hard time making decisions or stating opinions, particularly if there is a chance that it will disrupt the peace. Avoiding conflict is an integral motivation for Peacemakers. Nines also fear that they will push people away, which is why they often give in to the needs and desires of others. This can lead the Nine to feel resentful and actually push people away—the very thing they are trying to avoid.

Famous Peacemakers

Though we don't know what motivates other people, these are observational assessments. Let these guesses help you determine your own type.

James Taylor

Audrey Hepburn

Fred Rogers
("Mr. Rogers")

Jim Henson

Zooey Deschanel

Marie Kondo

STRESS AND SECURITY POINTS

When stressed, Enneagram Nines inherit the unhealthy qualities of a Six, the Loyalist. On the contrary, when healthy or in a place where they can achieve growth, they take on the positive qualities of a Three, the Achiever.

When stressed or not in a good place, Nines will exhibit the negative qualities of a Six, becoming more worried or anxious and spending time overthinking things that are out of their control. Nines will also become hyper focused on worst-case scenarios and will overplan to avoid them. When stressed, they often lack confidence.

When growing or in a good place, Nines take on the positive qualities of a Three. This may look like becoming extremely motivated and driven to get things done. They become extremely interested in the things that they are passionate about, and they want to set and achieve their goals. They are more confident and want to encourage others to be that way as well.

WINGS

Enneagram Nines have an Eight wing and a One wing. It's interesting because both Eight, the Challenger, and One, the Reformer, seem to be so different from a Nine, but the traits of those two types enhance the overall personality of a Nine.

Because Nines just want other people to be comfortable and happy, a Nine with a One wing is more focused on doing what is right for those people. They are more focused on justice, fairness, and making sure the rules are being followed. A Nine with a One wing may also be quieter than a Nine with an Eight wing, listening to all perspectives to get to the truth of the matter.

A Nine with an Eight wing may be more direct and assertive. They won't shy away from conflict as much as the stereotypical Nine. They may be more outspoken with their anger and more

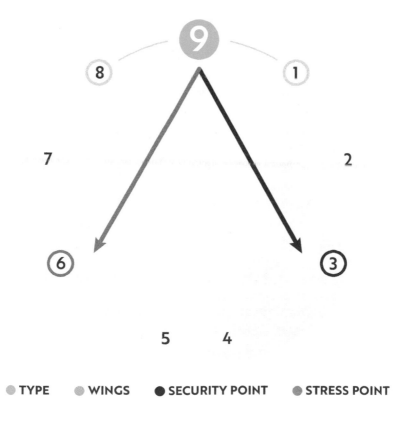

confident in who they are. A Nine with an Eight wing will exhibit a gentle strength, and they will use that strength to better the lives of others.

WHAT'S EASY FOR PEACEMAKERS

Peacemakers are naturals at, you guessed it, keeping the peace. They are always willing to mediate conflict and tense situations to return to a peaceful environment. They are the ones people go to when they need a nonjudgmental opinion and a listening ear. Nines are able to see all sides of a situation and have an ability to understand others like no other. It's easy for Nines to make friends because people genuinely enjoy being around them.

WHAT'S HARD FOR PEACEMAKERS

Addressing conflict head-on is something you typically won't find many Nines doing because they want to maintain peace in their relationships and environment. It's hard for Peacemakers to state their opinion or how they feel about something because they care more about other people being happy. Nines also struggle with making decisions and sticking to them. Because of their need to please others, Nines typically don't want to make a decision unless they know it will be well received.

HEALTHY BEHAVIORS

An Enneagram Nine's desire to maintain the peace around them inspires their acceptance and understanding of others. Because they want to dissipate conflict, they have developed a mediation skill set that allows them to hear all sides of a situation with empathy. Because of their desire to maintain that peace, Nines have perfected their communication skills, which start with listening first. They are patient with themselves and others, and they recognize that conflict is a part of life and can be solved with effective communication and empathy.

UNHEALTHY BEHAVIORS

Because of a Nine's strong need to avoid disruption in their peace, they may avoid anything that could create conflict or negative energy. Sometimes this looks like an inability to state their opinions or desires because of how others may interpret them, or it could look like being indecisive because they're afraid of disrupting the peace with their decision. Nines often feel like what they have to offer is not important, resulting in procrastination. Because they just want everyone to get along, they go along with others simply to keep the peace. This can lead to buried emotions and ultimately resentment when Nines feel ignored or taken advantage of.

WORK LIFE

Enneagram Nines in the workplace are steady, balanced, and committed to keeping the peace by maintaining a peaceful working environment and ensuring that relationships remain free of conflict. Nines try to play "devil's advocate" in workplace situations, and they will attempt to see all sides of the situation. Nines are very concerned with the workplace environment. It needs to be set up and decorated in a way that makes them feel comfortable. Nines may be quiet in the workplace, relying on others' opinions and thoughts instead of their own and even relying on colleagues to make decisions. This is because they believe their voice and opinions don't matter. If you are the coworker of a Nine, try to include them in the decision-making process, ask for their opinions, and encourage them to speak up. Remind them that their voice does matter.

FAMILY LIFE

Enneagram Nines are often the person in the family structure working to ensure that everyone is happy and getting along. They are called the Peacemaker for a reason. They want to maintain the peace in the family unit, as well as in every other area of their life. Nines have a calm presence that is typically contagious. Others are drawn to them for the comfort and understanding they provide. Nines feel extremely uncomfortable when it comes to family drama and conflict, making them unable to voice how they are feeling for fear of the potential negativity that it could create. This can turn into feelings of resentment that no one listens to them or takes their opinion into consideration. If you have a family member who is a Nine, let them make family decisions and voice their opinion and truly listen to what they have to say.

RELATIONSHIP LIFE

Enneagram Nines bring caring and peaceful qualities to a romantic relationship. They are great listeners and excel at offering advice because of their ability to see multiple perspectives. They are empathetic and just want to make sure that their partner is happy and well taken care of. However, as mentioned previously, they despise and avoid conflict, especially relationship conflict. This is because of their fear of separation. They fear doing something that makes them feel abandoned. Their fear of conflict can lead Nines to avoid anything that could be a potential issue, so they bury their true feelings. However, their feelings always come out, typically in a passive-aggressive way toward the people they care about the most. If you're in a relationship with a Nine, make sure that they know you aren't going anywhere, even if conflict occurs. Remind them that occasional conflict in a relationship is normal and that you will get through it together.

PEACEMAKERS AND OTHER ENNEAGRAM TYPES

Enneagram Nines tend to get along well with others because of their focus on creating a peaceful environment for everyone. Here are some dynamics you might see in relationships with an Enneagram Nine.

WITH ONES:
Nines and Ones understand each other because they are next to one another on the Enneagram. Nines can help show Ones how to be less critical of themselves, and Ones can help Nines take action.

WITH TWOS:
Nines and Twos are both nurturing and giving. They can show a great deal of compassion to one another, but they may struggle with boundaries and saying "no."

WITH THREES:
Threes and Nines are connected on the Enneagram and therefore can understand certain traits about each other. Nines can remind Threes to try to be more easygoing, and Threes can encourage Nines to stay motivated.

WITH FOURS:
Fours and Nines both focus on comfort and aesthetics, and they often pursue deep connections. Fours tend to be more aware of their emotions and feelings, whereas Nines may bury them to appease others. They can be extremely empathetic and understanding toward each other.

WITH FIVES:
Fives and Nines get along well because they both have a respect for space and boundaries. They are both intellectual and private at times. However, they may feel disconnected if they give each other too much space.

WITH SIXES:

Sixes and Nines can understand each other well because they are connected on the Enneagram. They both value security and guidance and offer that to one another. Nines are often a calming presence for Sixes.

WITH SEVENS:

Both Sevens and Nines typically have a positive outlook on life. They are optimistic and focused on relationships. Sevens can help Nines become more assertive and energetic.

WITH EIGHTS:

Eights and Nines can be total opposites at times, but they also balance each other out. Eights appreciate that Nines are nurturing and comforting; Nines appreciate that Eights are willing to stand up for them.

WITH NINES:

Two Nines offer each other immense patience, understanding, and care. They have an awareness about each other that others may not share. However, they may struggle with avoiding relational conflict and have a hard time making decisions.

Peacemaker Mantras

When things get tough or whenever you feel like it, repeat these mantras and affirmations out loud or in your head to help center yourself. You can repeat one or say them one after another.

- My thoughts and opinions matter.

- I make good decisions.

- I can put my happiness above others'.

- I am not responsible for another person's happiness.

- My feelings are important.

PEACEMAKER EXERCISE

The goal of this exercise is to encourage Nines to stay motivated and accomplish things on a daily basis. This can be difficult for Nines because they tend to feel overwhelmed when they have too much on their plate. However, by staying present, they can achieve whatever they set their minds to.

1. At the start of each day, list the things that absolutely need to get done during that day.

2. Number those things in order of importance. Consider what you need to do versus what someone else can do for you.

3. From this list, choose three things that you want to accomplish and break those down into more detailed to-do lists.

CLOSING

The Enneagram is a powerful tool you can use to increase your self-awareness and personal development. It can help you understand the motives and behaviors of the people in your life. Used correctly, the Enneagram is not an excuse for their behaviors but is instead an opportunity to grow into the person they truly want to be. The Enneagram shows you that although your motivations do not change, your understanding of these motivations can change drastically. With that understanding, you can offer yourself and others grace, compassion, and acceptance. And that is my wish for you.

RESOURCES

Online

EnneagramInstitute.com

TheEnneagramInBusiness.com

YourEnneagramCoach.com

Naranjo-SAT.com

InternationalEnneagram.org

Books

The Art of Typing: Powerful Tools for Enneagram Typing by Ginger Lapid-Bogda

The Complete Enneagram: 27 Paths to Greater Self-Knowledge by Beatrice Chestnut

The Enneagram for Relationships: Transform Your Connections with Friends, Family, Colleagues, and in Love by Ashton Whitmoyer-Ober, MA

Millenneagram: The Enneagram Guide for Discovering Your Truest, Baddest Self by Hannah Paasch

The Path Between Us: An Enneagram Journey to Healthy Relationships by Suzanne Stabile

The Road Back to You: An Enneagram Journey to Self-Discovery by Ian Morgan Cron and Suzanne Stabile

The Wisdom of the Enneagram: The Complete Guide to Psychological and Spiritual Growth for the Nine Personality Types by Don Richard Riso and Russ Hudson

Instagram

Abbey Howe @EnneagramWithAbbey

Amy Wicks @WholeheartedEnneagram

Beth McCord @YourEnneagramCoach

Enneagram and Coffee @SaraJaneCase

Enneagram Explained @EnneagramExplained

Kambrie Ross @Enneagram.Kam

Kim Eddy @ChristianEnneagram.Coach

Steph Barron Hall @NineTypesCo

REFERENCES

The Enneagram in Business. "Enneagram History and Theory." Accessed July 23, 2021. TheEnneagramInBusiness.com/the-enneagram/enneagram-history-and-theory/

The Enneagram Institute. "5: The Investigator." Accessed September 9, 2021. EnneagramInstitute.com/type-5

The Enneagram Institute. "The Traditional Enneagram." Accessed July 23, 2021. EnneagramInstitute.com/the-traditional-enneagram

The Naranjo Institute. "Dr. Claudio Naranjo." Accessed September 7, 2021. NaranjoInstitute.org.uk/naranjo.html

INDEX

ACKNOWLEDGMENTS

There are so many people to thank and, like always, I'm stressed about forgetting someone! I just want everyone to feel loved. Such an Enneagram Two thing. But I will give it a try.

First, I have to thank everyone at Callisto Media for continuing to give me an opportunity to share one of my passions with the world. Thank you to my editor, Eun H. Jeong, for your patience and your wealth of editing knowledge. It has been a joy to work with you.

To my Instagram community, my enneafans. I am eternally grateful for all of you for making this dream a reality. You show up every day wanting to learn, grow, and better understand yourself and others. I'm so proud of all of you.

To all my friends, who I have put on the back burner yet again while completing this manuscript, thank you for your understanding, love, and support of my dreams. I know that I can count on you to be my biggest fans.

To my mom, who stepped up and watched Preston when I needed to write and Derek needed to work, who has supported me day in, day out and taught me what it means to go after what I want in life. Who has simply just let me be me.

To the rest of my family, my siblings, and my in-laws. I could not have done this without your never-ending support. I know that it's hard to explain just what I do to other people, but you do a great job and I love you for it. Thank you for surrounding me with love.

Finally, Derek and Preston. You are my world and my reason for being. Derek, thank you for believing in me, for pushing me to feel confident in myself, for loving me unconditionally. And Preston, you've been in our lives for a short amount of time but you have changed everything about me. I don't remember life before you. I love you both more than words could ever express.

ABOUT THE AUTHOR

 **Ashton Whitmoyer-Ober, MA,** is a writer, public speaker, community psychologist, certified Enneagram coach, and advocate for the under-dog. She is a part-time professor and has her own Enneagram and life-coaching business, Enneagram Ashton. She is the author of *Enneagram for Relationships* and *The Two of Us: A Three-Year Couple's Journal*. Find her on Instagram @EnneagramAshton.